"To Seek a Newer World":

Bill Blackard

A HISTORY OF COLUMBIA COUNTY, GEORGIA

Gerald J. Smith, Ph.D.
Illustrated By William Clarence Blackard

Copyright 2001 © Gerald J. Smith
and
The Columbia County Historical Society

"To Seek a Newer World": A History of Columbia County
Gerald J. Smith, PH.D.

Copyright 2001 © Gerald J. Smith
and
The Columbia County Historical Society

Produced by
Southern Heritage Press
Murfreesboro, TN 37130

ISBN 1-889332-46-1 (Hardcover)

Library of Congress CIP Data In Progress

1.United States – History. Georgia. Columbia County.
2. Genealogy

Order books from:
Columbia County Historical Society
P.O. Box 325
Appling, Georgia 30802

CROSSING THE SAVANNAH RIVER ON A FERRY.

Illustrations by Bill Blackard

Book Layout and Design Tom Huckabee of
History Communications Associates

Photos courtesy of owners and
Images of America
Columbia County Georgia

DEDICATED
TO
THE MEMORY OF

JOSIE DOZIER

FOUNDER
AND
GUIDING SPIRIT
OF THE
COLUMBIA COUNTY
HISTORICAL SOCIETY

CONTENTS

INTRODUCTION

On the 23rd of August, 1929, the Georgia General Assembly, in preparation for Georgia Day, February 12, 1933, the two hundredth anniversary of the founding of the Colony of Georgia, requested each Judge of the Superior Courts in the state to charge their grand juries that a history of each county be prepared by that date in 1933. Further, the grand juries were to empower, or hire, a suitable person as county historian to do this thing. These histories were to be deposited in the State's Department of Archives and History for information for historians, genealogists, biographers and so on. Consequently, many county histories appeared in 1933, and many have appeared since.

These "official" histories contained much information which had been gleaned from old newspapers, diaries, reminiscences, legend, hearsay, and perhaps a little bit of gossip. They tended to be overloaded with deeds, wills, marriage records and even excerpts from family Bibles. Each was particularly heavy on the War Between The States era, with close attention given to those gallant lads who served in the companies raised in that county. The leading families in the counties each had their own separate write-up, sent in by the family's historian. Most of the cemeteries of the county were included, many with each deceased person listed, especially those men who had died in battle in the nation's conflicts.

While these books hold a wealth of information for today, critically, one is compelled to say that these "official" histories had serious flaws which a county history of today would wish to avoid:

1.   They were very and perhaps by design exclusive. They were "whites only" histories, which reflected the white supremacy philosophy of that time. Not only that, they were elitist whites of the old Southern aristocracy, paying some attention, to be fair to the white middle class, but none to the white yeoman class. The caste system, as tight as anything Hinduism ever produced, was

still in vogue, maybe more so since many outsiders had come into the counties since "The War." The African American people were conspicuously absent in these histories, except for a mention every now and then of some revered "Aunt Lukey" or "Uncle Joe."

2.   Because much of the material was taken from legend, family lore, and hearsay of other forms, myths were recorded and perpetuated in these books, the very publication of which myths rendered them authoritative and permanent.

3.   The appendices of these histories fairly bulged with cemetery records of the white churches and families, wills, deeds, court cases, and marriage records. Now, given that information was much more difficult to acquire then than it is now, it was necessary for the official document of the county's past to have these appendices. As we know, these days, we have to "prove" we were born to obtain a portion of our Social Security money; all of these information sources, plus church records, are very necessary thereto. As we now live in the age of information because of cyber-technology, we can go to the computer's search engines and get the same information in much less time and with considerably less bother.

4.   In many instances, these histories were not systematically organized but instead presented a hodgepodge of information which the reader had to endeavor to sort out. One reason for this may be the time-line within which the historian had to work, with a dead-line to meet which was a bicentennial celebration of the state's genesis.

For whatever reason, at the time the official county histories appeared, none was written about Columbia County. One person indeed suggested when asked about this peculiarity that in 1933, there was not much to write about in Columbia County! This was spoken in jest, however, for this county has a distinguished and important place in the development of the state and the nation. Several attempts have been made to produce a county chronicle, the largest being the History of Columbia County at the time of the nation's bicentennial in 1976. This attempt was basically a collection of newspaper articles, short historical narratives about salient points, and copies of official documents. Smaller books have appeared like <u>Historical Landmarks and Legends of</u> <u>Columbia County</u>, which also was prepared in honor of the bicentennial by the County Historical Society. Michael White's <u>Columbia County: a Study of Its Streams, Rivers, and Historic</u> <u>Water Mill Sites </u>(1998) is a very useful book, particularly of the natural resources of the county.   Jeanette Kelley's books, <u>Columbia County – A Study Guide</u> and <u>Our Heritage:</u> <u>Personalities 1754 –1983</u>, and Charles Lord's many articles in local newspapers are very informative, as is the Martinez-Evans Jaycees' <u>Columbia County, Then and Now</u> (no date). Several websites are now available, also.

Three excellent church histories have been published which also contain very good peripheral information about other churches, towns, et cetera. Harris and Mosteller's work on Kiokee Baptist Church is one of the most comprehensive this writer has ever read. The Abilene Baptist history is also quite inclusive. Kathy Ruddy's history of the Grovetown Methodist Church development is also a fine study of the growth of the town of Grovetown. Other church histories, not as long as the above, were also very useful and welcomed. A good, solid publication on all the churches of the county would be a worthy project for someone. In the same vein, a good published article on the <u>Columbia</u> <u>Sentinel</u> would be useful. A very fine and concise history of Harlem by Patricia Moore is "hidden" in a zip code directory compiled in 1976 by the North Harlem Elementary PTA.

This present history has attempted to be as objective as possible in covering the significant events which shaped the county. No attempt has been made, consciously anyway, to show favoritism to any particular family, only insofar as historical importance warranted. For example, no history of this county would be complete without dealing with the contributions of the Few family, the Mercers, and most certainly the Daniel Marshall clan.

The African American experience, so very real and significant in the county, has been presented, particularly in regards to the vexing Reconstruction era and its fall-out in Negro education, politics, and well-being. The Native American experience, with its wealthy prehistoric legacy, is dealt with. Both these groups deserve a much longer and authoritative treatment in published form.

No attempt has been made to give a history of each of the many churches and businesses in the county today. Only those of historic importance are herein. Salient points of the histories of the towns and communities, not complete chronicles, are given.

This writer has endeavored to make the best informed decision about some vexing questions, based on comparison of texts available and, perhaps, intuition:

1. The location of Brandon--this settlement has been banded about as absorbed by Wrightsborough, abandoned by the settlers, et cetera. A 1779 map, however, shows it plainly and separately from Wrightsborough.

2. "Quaker Settlements" has been located variously in the upcountry around Wrightsborough or as synonymous with Quaker Springs near Augusta. I chose the latter.

3. The courthouse saga is determined as best I can by comparing and contrasting sources.

History is a curious thing indeed, for the very moment one types the word itself, it has already become "history." As the good Romans used to say, TEMPUS FUGIT (Time Flees) and TEMPUS EDAX (Time Devours); therefore, the writing of a history could go on and on. Pope Julius asked of Michaelangelo of the painting of the ceiling of the Sistine Chapel, "When will you make an end?" After many months of research and thought, this writer finally had to ask himself the same question. The answer was to stop and start writing, for a history of this type is of its own nature one which is open-ended. Columbia County is a living thing, growing more and more every day, and promises to do so for a long time to come, so this history does not claim to be definitive.

I wish to thank and acknowledge the help of several persons, the first being Dr. Edward Cashin, who suggested, for whatever motive, that I do this thing; William "Bill" and Jean Blackard, who have gone an extra mile or two to help in research and to point out items of significant value; Charles Lord, whose friendship and enthusiasm about the county's past, has been much needed; Mrs. Mary Sanders for help in the education section of the book; Ms. Kathy B. Ruddy for the history of the Grovetown Methodist charge and of Grovetown; Lallie Dozier Benkoski for avidly collecting many photos and published items and putting the same at my disposal; Kenneth Sassaman and Daniel Elliott for offering much archaeological material; local church historians; Gibbs Library, Augusta State University Library, Paine College Library, and the Columbia County Historical Society; all were most cordial and helpful; and my wife Rebecca, for patience and understanding.

I should make mention especially of the sub-committee of the Historical Society who read the manuscript and offered very timely suggestions: Patricia Moore, Joe Tankersly, and William Blackard. They saved me from several embarrassments!

Finally, it is hoped the reader will find something of note herein. To use the Great Apostle's admonition, though, after the reader has read this book, "if there be any virtue, if there be any praise, think on these things!"

—Chapter One—

*G*eography and

*F*irst *I*nhabitants

Land grant by King George III that can be found today in the Robert Lane hone. (Courtesy of Lallie Dozier Benkoski.)

Geographically, Columbia County (over 300 square miles) lies three-fourths in the Georgia Piedmont and one-fourth in the Coastal Plain. The Fall-line or Sand Hills represents the division marker. The Savannah River begins in the Piedmont and passes by the county forming her eastern boundary.

The Fall Line, where the geologic distinctions of the Piedmont (metamorphic and igneous rock) pass under the Coastal Plain, is seen in the Savannah River as small rapids, the water lapping the rocks which cut across its current. The Fall Line also marks the navigable boundary of the river from Columbia County to Savannah, Georgia. The river is fed by many tributaries in the County, the principal ones being Kiokee, Euchee, and Keg Creeks.

Geologically, the County lies within the Appalachian Mobile Belt and on the Belair and Augusta fault zones. Other subterranean features are the Donoho Creek Formation, the Huber Foundation, Dry Branch Formation, Tobacco Road Formation, Altamaha Foundation, and Appling Granite Pluton. The latter is represented prominently in the County by Heggies Rock near Appling, a nature preserve:

> The 100-acre rock, towering nearly 150 feet above the forest floor, is an obscure link in an evolutionary chain that began with a volcanic eruption 220 million years ago. The geologic oddity, with terrain more like Arizona than east Georgia, was formed when molten rock was thrust upward through the Earth's crust in what now is Columbia County. [1]

Heggie Rock near Appling, c1985. (Courtesy of Pat Blanchard.)

Named for Archibald Heggie, an early County resident, the phenomenon has "rare, or endangered, plants studied by botanists nationwide .. ." [2] The rock formation is a part of the granite stratum which cuts through the state Piedmont region. Another granite source, Smith's Rock, is currently being quarried. Stone Mountain near Atlanta is the most noted of these outcroppings. Other prominent elevations in the County are Burks Mountain and Mount Carmel (also known as Little Mountain), respectively 460 feet and 540 feet above sea level. Certainly not mountains in the strict sense, these prominences are characteristic of the Piedmont. Indeed, Harlem is 535 feet above sea level.

The greatest geological feature at present in the County is the Strom Thurmond Lake, known to Georgia residents fondly as Clark Hill, which inundates the northeastern corner. The County has 120 of the 1200 miles of shoreline. The dam for this huge 70,000 acre watershed is located in the County. "The hydroelectric power generated by the dam has become one of the most important aspects of the Thurmond Lake project."[3] Mistletoe State Park on the lake near the McDuffie County line is a a significant tourist and natural resource as it protects much flora and fauna while offering great recreation facilities.

The topography of the County "consists mostly of broad to narrow, very gently sloping ridgetops and long to short sloping and moderately steep hillsides adjacent to numerous small drainageways that dissect the area."[4] Most of the subdivision development in the Martinez-Evans area has tended to preserve these features, but the rural areas of the County truly reflect the natural beauty of the topography. As old farmers said about the county, "Hit lays a'rolling."

The soils of the County's Piedmont section are classified as Georgeville-Wedowee (loamy or sandy); Wedowee-Cecil (loamy or sandy); and Cecil-Appling-Wedowee (loamy and sandy). In the Sand Hills or Coastal Plain portion are Wagram-Troup-Norfolk (sandy surface and loamy subsoil) and Chewacia-Toccoa-Wehadkee (loamy). [5]

3

The climate of the County brings long hot summers, periods of drought, and great humidity. Winters are milder than in the past when, as the older generation remembers, hog killings and syrup-making occurred around Thanksgiving Day when heavy frosts began. Although January is the coldest month on average, snow is very rare except for heavy winter fronts which effect the entire Southeast. In the last few decades, the seasons of the year have tended to blend into two--cool to moderate and very hot.

Rainfall is scarce in the months of July and August, necessitating water rationing for lawns and gardens in the high-density populated suburban areas. Humidity averages 60-65% annually but is often much more significant. Thunderstorms are the predominant rainmakers in the summer months, bringing with them lightning and hail damage. Tornadoes are fortunately rare, but the County has experienced at times the fringes of the larger Atlantic and Gulf hurricanes. Subsequent flooding has occurred in some suburban areas.

The dearth of heavy freezing on the soil levels in the County encourages a plethora of insect pests--mosquitoes, roaches, beetles, et cetera. The ground does not freeze hard enough to kill their larvae, and summer brings them out in abundance. Fire-ants are also more than a nuisance to homeowners and farmers alike. The mild weather has welcomed also a newcomer to the County's fauna--the humble armadillo.

The County's growth is nowhere better seen than in its population explosion. In 1950, the total population of all the counties contiguous to Lake Thurmond numbered 67,203; 9,525 in Columbia County. By 1990, Columbia County alone had grown to 66,000. Today, its inhabitants number in excess of 92,000 due to the influx of businesses, the overall excellence of its schools, and its attractive landscape. The Lake and Fort Gordon have brought many retirees to the County as well as the ready availability of medical care.

The urbanization, which has attended the increase of population, has had a radical effect on the County's agriculture and farming. In 1919, there were 1,914 farms in the County, for the most part tenant-run. The cash crop was cotton as in antebellum days when large plantations sprawled over the area. Tobacco was also grown. Today, there are only three fulltime farms, one dairy and two beef-cattle. Those farms which are run on a part-time basis, that is, not self-supporting, number 154. These are cattle, hay, and horse farms.

The natural resources in the County provide industry: timber, mining firms, and well water. Pollard's Lumber Company remains the largest timber operation. The gravel quarry near Appling, Knox-Rivers, also employs many. The John Deere Company and many others near Grovetown are new industries.

The variegated flora and fauna and minerals of the County are given in the appendix. Much of the animal life is found in the Lake Thurmond vicinity and is protected by the U.S. Army Corps of Engineers or in Mistletoe State Park by the State Department of Natural Resources. The inherent beauty of both flora and fauna is an asset to the County.

The First Inhabitants

Around 15,000 B.C., prehistoric hunters following their prey left evidences of their passage through the Central Savannah River Area (CSRA) in the many campsites along the Savannah River and its tributaries. Known as Paleoindians, they left distinctive signatures in their implements of stone: Clovis, Cumberland, Quad, and Dalton points, drills, scrapers, and knives. Nomadic perforce, they subsisted on large and small game, fish, and fruits and nuts.[6] This all seems strange to modern Americans, but as archaeologist Kenneth Sassaman wrote,"Compared to the hubbub and stress of the modern world to which we belong, the hunting and gathering way of life seems to have been more simple and gentle."[7] They died of various causes, but hypertension was not one of them.

Circa 8,000 B.C., as the Paleo period moved into the Archaic (8,000-1,000 B.C.), the hunter-gatherer mode of existence began a slow but perceptible change as important environmental alterations occurred. The flora and fauna became over the centuries essentially like it is today, and the ecosystem settled into more predictable patterns of weather and seasons of the year. The human inhabitants apparently liked what they saw in the Savannah River valley and began to settle down along the ridges overlooking the River or on its islands. During this period, the use of food

6

containers, the development of polished and ground tools and ornaments of stone, bone and shell, and the appearance of more permanent dwellings marked a shift in the indigenous lifestyle of the people.[8]

They saw the abundance of fish in the waterways and made acquaintance with the freshwater shellfish known as the mussel.

> They had discovered that an almost inexhaustible supply of these prolific creatures was to be had for the taking... Perhaps the taste for this form of diet was difficult to acquire, but once achieved it freed them for generations from the hard necessity of moving their camp every time the game grew scarce.[9]

Supplementing their riverine diet with woodland game such as deer, bear, and turkey, the nomads settled down. Their trash heaps of shell, middens, grew as generations added to the refuse. Archaeologists have found these middens all over the CSRA. Some were eventually used as convenient burial places as well as for the bases of later and more elaborate ceremonial mounds such as seen in the Ocmulgee National Site near Macon, Georgia.

In Columbia County, over 30 prehistoric sites are to be found. The most significant of these, which has attracted international attention, is located on Stallings Island. The mound there, containing many burials, also shows evidence of a distinct culture which flourished around 2,000 B.C. The Stallings Culture, named for the island, was widespread in the region and as Sassaman wrote, "was indeed innovative. It included the first shell fishing, the first pottery, and the first settled community life..."[10]

The Mill Branch Culture in Warren County had already developed a rudimentary pottery, but it was the Stallings Culture which first introduced an elaborate pottery tempered with Spanish moss, and a lifestyle which was unique.

> The pottery, for instance, is decorated elaborately with punctations and incisions. Carved bone pins sport a variety of concentric designs. Their clothing and hair designs were perhaps just as distinctive. There probably was no mistaking a Stallings person. [11]

7

Cooked in their pottery were vegetables such as squash, sunflower and maize, which were a part of their diet as well as meat, fish, and the ever-abundant nuts and berries.

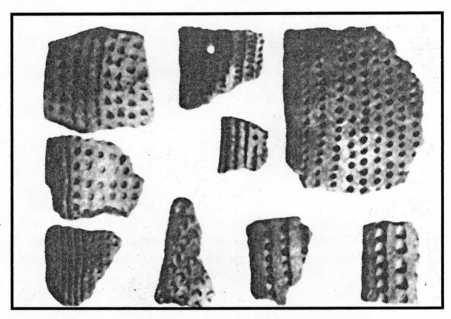

Prehistoric shards from Stallings Island show the peculiar "drag and jab" method of decoration. This is the first pottery in North America and is dated 2400-2200 B.C. (Courtesy of G.J. Smith.)

Archaeologists are still studying the Stallings Island mound and environs. Skeletons exhumed there reflect a belief in the afterlife and to the surprise of early archeologists in this century, also reflected a sophisticated use of medicine – one of the skulls revealed a primitive but definite form of brain surgery or trephanning! [12]

Another Columbia County prehistoric site is the excavation known as the Victor Mills site on the river bluffs near the present Lock and Dam. The evidence there has connected it with the Stallings Culture, but earlier in its history.[13] The Lake Springs Site, excavated in 1951, yielded besides period artifacts, eleven skeletons of prehistoric persons, which are now in the Smithsonian Institution. These people belonged to the pre-Stallings Culture in the Early Archaic Period.[14]

The Stallings Culture only lasted about two centuries. The causes of its decline are still being debated by Sassaman and his colleagues. He maintains, however, that "the Stallings Culture represents the highest order of cultural elaboration and integration ever witnessed in 9000 years of local hunter-gatherer prehistory."[15] Such is no mean commendation of a Native American phenomenon which belongs uniquely to Columbia County.

During the Woodland and Mississippian Periods (1,000 B.C. - 1600 A.D.), evidence of occupation in the County is seen in a site at the mouth of Kiokee Creek where pottery sherds indicate that the Swift Creek Culture of southwest Georgia and Florida indeed had some influence. Its complicated-stamped pottery designs are a hallmark of that culture, and these designs have been found in the county.[16]

At least five other mounds are located on Euchee and Kiokee Creeks, some on the Pollard property along the Savannah River. To what prehistoric culture they belonged has not been determined. On Little Mountain (Mount Carmel) is a frog effigy of stones which undoubtedly is prehistoric in origin.

Along Kiokee Creek near Appling, abundant evidence has been found of multi-cultural occupation of the same sites. One such has yielded Clovis artifacts (11,500 years ago), Taylor and Palmer points (10,000 years old), Dalton implements (8000 years ago) and Morrow Mountain tools (5,000 years old), all of which preceded Stallings Island Culture by many centuries. Pottery remains there indicate, however, a strong Stallings presence along with its signature tools, nut stones, soapstone slabs, knives, bannerstones and points. Triangular points and gorgets found there show that later Woodland and Mississippian cultures used the site. Clay-lined firepits have yielded a variety of food debris (shells, fowl and animal bones) but no human remains have been found. The speculation is that perhaps the dead may have been interred on Stalling's Island, twelve miles away.

The site has also yielded very unusual quartz tanged knives which seem to be of the Morrow Mountain type, thus predating the Stallings people. Also a point unique to the archeologists is named Kiokee Creek Stemmed. Further expert exploration of the length of Kiokee and Euchee Creeks, as well as the other tributaries in the county, will perhaps reveal a very rich prehistory not yet examined. Artifacts indeed have been found on many of these smaller creeks. The presence of mounds indicates a fairly strong occupation by the Woodland people. Caves near Grovetown have also borne evidence of prehistory.

Around 1450 A.D., the inhabitants vacated the Columbia County area for about two centuries. As Anderson writes, "The abandonment of the central and lower Savannah was caused by a combination of factors, of which changes in environmental conditions and in the regional political landscape were perhaps the most important."[17] The rise of powerful chiefdoms coupled with droughts and famine appear to be the chief culprits. Whatever the reason, radiocarbon dating of artifacts has found no appreciable human occupation in the county for that period. Moreover, when Hernando de Soto trekked through the eastern part of the state in 1540, he found no residents in the Central Savannah Area.

Sometime around 1650, the Uchee (Yuchi) Indians migrated from the Appalachia into the County and environs. By the time of the founding of the Georgia Colony in 1733, the Uchees considered themselves the most ancient of the Native Americans in the area. The Dutchman, Philip von Reck observed of them:

The Indians (Yuchi) are of moderate stature, robust and strong. Their skin is black-yellow, .. They color their faces with all sorts of colors, especially black shaded with red ... They wear no beards and they tear out what little bit does grow ... they cover themselves with a short blanket ... the women are completely clothed ... [18]

KING OF THE YUCHIS, SENKAITSCHI

They proved to be good neighbors to the erstwhile Europeans, even serving with Oglethorpe against the Spanish. Reverend John Wesley, however, Oglethorpe's spiritual advisor and sometime missionary to the natives, was not impressed favorably with the Uchees. Wrote he, "They are indeed hated by most and despised by all the other nations as well for their cowardice as their superlative diligence in thieving and for out-lying all the other Indians on the Continent."[19] Mr. Wesley, who had not met all the other Indians on the Continent, was generally soured by Europeans and Indians alike before he returned contritely to England and could hardly be objective in his statement about the Euchees.

The Uchees spoke a language all their own, unlike those of other tribes, but classified as Muskogean.[20] It was a very guttural, unpolished tongue, the most difficult, according to a contemporary linguist, to adapt to English orthography than any other Indian language. The Uchees, for example, learned the Creek tongue, but the Creeks could never master the Uchee.[21] Apparently, they had little concern for who could or could not handle their language, for they clung stubbornly to their customs and beliefs.

Their religion in particular reflected a sophistication which was characteristic of all the Southeastern tribes. The good Mr. Wesley was no doubt taken aback when he inquired of the ancient chief Chicoli why he thought he was made as a human. The reply was illuminating:

> He that is above knows what he has made us for. We know nothing. We are in the dark. But white men know much. And yet white men build great houses as if they were to live forever. But white men cannot live forever. In a little time, white men will be dust as well as I.[22]

A Glossary of Yuchi & Creek Words

Yuchee	Creek	English
Iz-ag-tscka	Tag-lo	Mullet
Tschi-pa-ke	--	Garfish
Jonto	--	Acorn
Tap-ap-te-ha	Hal-pa-ta	Alligator
Saa	--	Snake
Fekasaanika	--	Bull snake
Hatsheleitschi	--	Tail
Zishagzafen	Wajo	Flying squirrel
Zozassi	Fu-zat-ta	Redbird
--	Jo-wei-ka	Bluebird
U-i-fossoa	Zoskela	Waterbird
Setan	Sa-ki-la	Blackbird
Senon	--	Bird
Tsee	Ta-si	Bluejay
Tawegzene	Ta-fo-lope	Butterfly
--	Wa-ko	Crane
--	Ko-tot-ka	Squash
Jonschipi	--	Walnut
Tschas-cispi	--	Black
Yaking-ka	--	Tree
--	Katalsch-pa	Catalpa
Za-ta-fo-lot-ka	--	Tea
--	Is-ti	Person
Satontschi	--	Maypop
Tahasha	Ossana	Otter
Sa-tat-a	--	Parakeet
Zuntshcipa	Pat-schi	Dove

NOTE: Von Reck gives these sounds in his native German but still shows the difference in the Yuchi and Creek words. The Creek is certainly the easier of the two.

The Yuchis and the Appalachee Indians, who had moved up from Florida, declined in the area, however, when they allied against the powerful Creek nation and were defeated. Many of them were enslaved by the Creeks, their land was ceded to the colonists, so most migrated to western Georgia to settle along the Chattahoochee and Flint Rivers. The word Chattahoochee comes from the Yuchi language. Later, with the great, ignominious removal of the Georgia tribes to Oklahoma, the Yuchi left the state except for some small enclaves near Columbus, Georgia. In Columbia County, their legacy is maintained in Euchee and Kiokee Creeks and in the "Old Fields" near the river which they had settled and cultivated.

In the southern part of the county was located the Upper Trading Path which is now Highway 78 to a great extent. The historical marker near Harlem reads:

> For the last twenty miles, this highway has followed the course of the noted Upper Trading Path that led from present Augusta to Indian tribes as far away as the Mississippi River. By various connections the trail reached the Cherokees of North Georgia; the Muscogees or Creeks of Eastern Alabama; and the Choctaws and Chickasaws of Northern Mississippi. The Oakfuskee Path, main branch of the route, led past Warrenton, Griffin, and Greenville to Oakfuskee Town, an early Upper Creek center, on the Tallapoosa River in Alabama. White traders began using this trail in the early 1700's.

The Lower Trade Path went southwest through what is now Fort Gordon. In truth, (see map p. 25) many of the roadways in use today throughout the state follow the old routes laid down by the Indians.

The best epitaph of the Native American presence in the South is that by Charles Hudson, including as it does, the proud Uchees:

> The native people of the American South--the Southeastern Indians--possessed the richest culture of any of the native people north of Mexico. It was richest by almost any measure. At the time Europeans first came to the New World, the Southeastern Indians lived on the fruits of an

economy which combined farming with hunting and gathering; they organized themselves into relatively complex political units; they built large towns and monumental ceremonial centers; and they possessed a rich symbolism and an expressive art style.[23]

It must be mentioned here on behalf of these original peoples that development and current vandalism of prehistoric mounds and campsites are constant threats to on-going attempts to understand the earliest inhabitants and their lore.

Chapter One Footnotes

[1]Reed Wicander and James Monroe, <u>Historical Geology:</u> <u>Evolution Of The Earth And Life In Time</u> (New York: West, 1989), 258 ff. For Heggies Rock quote, Dan Marshall "Rare Plants Thrive at Heggies Rock," <u>Albany (Ga) Herald</u>, 1999. H.R. Casey, a planter-physician in Columbia County in the 1800's, describes the social outings to Heggies Rock, <u>Columbia Sentinel</u>, March 28. 1883.

[2]Marshall.

[3] <u>Cultural Resources Survey, Thurmond Lake, Mcduffie And Columbia Counties</u>, 1976, 64.

[4] <u>Soil Survey Of Columbia, Mcduffie And Warren Counties</u> (Washington, D.C.: USDA, 1967), 21.

[5]Ibid.

[6]Sharyn Kane and Richard Keaton, <u>Beneath These Waters</u> (National Park Service, 1993), 15.

[7]"Stallings: The Rise and Fall of a Hunting and Gathering Society," <u>Legacy I</u> (July 1996), 6.

[8]Charles Hudson, <u>The Southeastern Indians</u> (Knoxville: University of Tennessee Press, 1976), 52-54

[9]G.D. Pope, Jr. <u>Ocmulgee</u> (Washington: National Park Service #24), 13. See also <u>Beneath These Waters</u>, 53-54.

[10]Sassaman, 4-5

[11]Sassaman, 7.

[12]William Claflin, Jr., "The Stalling's Island Mound," Peabody Museum Papers XIV (New York: Kraus, 1922), 12-13. <u>Cultural Resources Survey, 41</u>.

[13]Sassaman, 13.

[14] Charles Miller, "The Lake Springs Site Columbia County," <u>American Antiquities 15</u>, 438-519; Robert R. Steiner, "Prehistoric Settlement Big Kiokee Creek," American Association for the Advancement of Science Proceedings (1899), 379-382. Robert Roland Steiner was an eminent archeologist from Columbia County. One of his letters is in the Grovetown Museum, donated by Charles Lord.

[15]Sassaman, 13.

[16]Daniel Elliott, "Archaeology and Historical Geography of the Savannah River Floodplain near Augusta, Georgia," <u>Laboratory Of Archaeology Series</u> Report No. 22. Athens: University of Georgia, 1981. Charles Colcock Jones, Jr., in his <u>Antiquities Of The Southern Indians, Particularly Of The Georgia Tribes </u>(New York:Appleton, 1873), 337, mentions a large village site of the Woodland Period at the mouth of Big Kiokee Creek on the Savannah River. Unfortunately, flooding has erased any vestiges.

[17] David Anderson, <u>The Savannah River Chiefdoms </u>(Tuscaloosa: University of Alabama Press, 1994), 326-327.

[18]Christian Hvidt, ed. <u>Von Reck's Voyage</u> (Savannah: Beehive Press, 1990), 40.

[19]Hugh Martin, ed. <u>Selections From The Journal Of John Wesley</u> (London: S.C.M. Press, 1955), 20.

[20]Hudson, 23.

[21]Hudson, 24. James M. Crawford, "Yuchi Phonology," <u>International Journal Of American Linguistics 39 </u>(1973), 173-179.

[22]Martin, 21.

[23]Hudson, 3. As a note of interest old Yuchi Town, an archaeological site on the Fort Benning Reservation, Russell

County, Alabama, was placed on the National Register of Historic Places, June 19, 1996. Descendants of the Yuchi Tribe were honored guests at the ceremony.

—Chapter Two—

Part I

*U*nion to *D*isunion

The first European presence along Kiokee and Euchee Creeks and Little River was that of the hardy fur trapper-frontiersman who sought pelts of various animals for profit. Before the Georgia Colony was ever conceived, white men from Virginia and South Carolina moved down the Savannah River or came up from Florida, made friends with the Indians or ignored them, and set their traps. Early on, these men exterminated the venerable bison, a large beast which had a pelt "too heavy for the strongest man to lift from the ground. . .," as naturalist Mark Catesby wrote about his travels to the area in 1722.[1]

Over time deer, otter, beaver and raccoon pelts, along with cattle skins, were brought down the Savannah River and sold to export merchants in the new town of Augusta. The traffic in skins thus became a great asset: "In the height of the season as many as 600 white traders with 2000 pack horses laden with deer and otter skins came here to engage in their traffic."[2]

So then, when Georgia became a royal colony in 1752, the northern part of St. Paul's Parish which later became Columbia County was still a frontier albeit the European was surely no stranger to the area. To number the inhabitants of the entire colony of Georgia at 20,000 of all races was hyperbole; trade and commerce were sparse—150 or so ships a year put in at Savannah, the main port. Manufacture was virtually non-existent.

Still, what Georgia's people lacked in these areas was compensated for by great energy and elan. Royal Governor James Wright wrote in 1766:

> Their Whole strength and attention is employed in planting Rice, Indigo, Corn, & Pease, and a small quantity of Wheat and Rye, in making pitch, tar, turpentine, shingles & staves, in sawing lumber & scantlings, boards of every kind,-and in raising stocks of Cattle, Mules, and Hogs. [3]

All this bustle boded well for the new Colony, for it indicated that Georgia could be a place of great promise, especially up the Savannah River around Fort Augusta.

In 1763, at the close of the French and Indian War, it was determined that the Georgia Colony could settle whites as far as Little River, twenty miles above Augusta. The authorities were very generous with giving away to settlers the erstwhile land of the Native Americans. The Headright System was used in which a single man could get 100 acres of land and if he married, an extra 100 acres. If he already had a family, he could acquire from the largesse of the Crown 100 acres for himself, 50 acres for his spouse and 50 extra for each child, slave, and indentured servants. He could not get, however, over 1000 acres total. Generosity does have its limits, it seems. Still, the average land grant was not over 300 acres. [4]

The first settlers to arrive in what became Columbia County were a party of Quakers under Edmund Gray in 1751. They established a village named Brandon on the Little River. Because of an altercation between Gray and Governor John Reynolds, the settlers were forced to leave.[5] A 1779 map still shows the village. On July 3, 1770, a grant was issued to "Joseph Maddock and Jonathon Sell ... This was the first and earliest grant issued for land in the township of Wrightsborough."[6] The town had been laid out in 1768 and began to grow as settlers, most of whom were not Quakers, moved in. The road ordered in 1769 to run from there to Fort Augusta, appropriately named Wrightsborough Road, was finished in 1770. Quaker Road was built from there to Savannah. Another community, Friendsborough, was settled in 1776 near Wrightsborough.

The settlers were an industrious lot indeed. They came from Pennsylvania, Maryland, Virginia, North Carolina – tough stock, inured to difficulty, educated, self-respecting, and independent to a fault. These upcountry newcomers were the cream of the crop. The region was described thus by Dr. Thomas Taylor to a friend in January 1776:

> As you approach this Settlement (Wrightsborough) the Land is much richer & diversified with Hills and Dales. The Country too is more populous, most of the Settlers having arrived within this eight years from the back parts of Pennsylvania and Virginia. The land here bears pretty good Wheat, Rye, Oats, Pease, Indian Corn, Indigo, Cotton, & Peaches are pretty plentiful but no other Fruit, merely (I believe) for Want of Culture. The Woods hereabouts consist of short-leav'd Pine, Oak & hiccory.[7]

The news was soon out that the upcountry or backcountry of St. Paul's Parish was lush with game of every sort for the taking; overrunning with arable soil which could grow everything but money on trees; all-in-all, offering opportunities for growth in many areas. Tobacco soon became the big crop with great

21

containers called "Hogsheads" being rolled down to Augusta or transported on rafts down the Savannah River.

TOBACCO NOTE

_____River

_____Warehouse, the_____day of_____, 179–

Mark.	No.	Oronoko			Sweet Scented Leaf			Stemmed Leaf		
		Gross.	Tare.	Net.	Gross.	Tare.	Net.	Gross.	Tare.	Ne

Received of_____, _____hogshead of cr‹ tobacco, marks, numbers, weight, and species as per above, to ‹ delivered by us to the said_____for exportatio when demanded.

Witness our hands, the_____day of_____, 179—.

TRANSFER NOTE

_____River

_____Warehouse, the_____ day of_____.

Received of_____, _____pounds of trar fer tobacco, to be delivered on demand to him or his order.

But there were the Native Americans, always the thorn or serpent in the new Garden of Eden or New Canaan, as so many displaced pilgrims from Europe liked to call the New World. The Creek Indians especially were at times peaceful as can be, but at other times, when aroused, they could be murderously bent. The old saying, "The good Lord willing and the Creek don't rise (pronounced riz)" had nothing to do with tributaries or water. It was a reference to a common threat to all settlers. The country was still largely wilderness and in bad times, there was literally a Creek behind every tree! Every community perforce had its blockhouse or fortified house in which the townsfolk could gather when the Creeks "riz."

There were numerous accounts of white families being massacred or communities being attacked, as with the experience at Quaker Springs, a settlement between Wrightsborough and Augusta. Adiel Sherwood wrote in 1829: "Quaker Springs, a small cluster of houses on the Washington road, 7 m. from Augusta. Here a settlement was made by the Quakers in 1750; but they were alarmed by the murders committed by the Cherokees (Creeks actually), and fled." [8]

But the settlers kept coming, despite all threats and Indians. In the early 1770's, Reverend Daniel Marshall led another band to the Kiokee Creek area above Augusta about 15 miles from Wrightsborough. These were Separate Baptists from South Carolina who like so many were seeking a place remote where they could worship and live with impunity, Marshall established a meetinghouse named first simply  Kiokee in 1772, which later became Kiokee Baptist Church, the first Baptist church in Georgia.[9]

Several miles northwest of Kiokee, another group of settlers established the Cobbham (pronounced Cobb-ham) community. Near this, Thomas Brown set up his plantation-village in the 1770's which he named, to no one's surprise, Brownsborough. His indentured servants, over 36 in number, with their families, built the settlement as he planned. This community was to have an important place in subsequent developments. [10] The upcountry of St. Paul's Parish thus grew swiftly by the time of the Revolution, with such families as the Fews, Baldwins, and Marshalls. Their influence politically was apparently such that the first voting in the

Parish was done at Kiokee Meetinghouse in 1777. But more of that later.

The settlers were keenly aware of events transpiring on a grander scale, for as newcomers came in, they brought news of a growing dissatisfaction with the Crown which some espoused or a deep love for the King. These two sentiments could not mix and a small dark cloud appeared on the deep blue horizon of their hopes and dreams which boded much evil to come,

Most of the settlers were satisfied with British rule, for the army kept the Creeks at bay, so 74 citizens of the upcountry wrote letters to the <u>Georgia Gazette</u> newspaper protesting the actions of the zealots who were agitating for action against the King. The American Revolution, then, brought to the upcountry a period of suffering that was not easily forgotten. Friends parted over following the King (Tory, Loyalist) or rebelling to claim independence from Great Britain (Whig Patriot).

As in all circumstances involving politics, emotion often took the upper hand and reason forsaken. Hotheads for independence, Sons of Liberty or Liberty Boys, took all before them and did not look back. Their zeal made a powerful enemy out of Thomas Brown when he was tarred, feathered and tortured by some of them on August 2, 1775. He earned a sobriquet "Burnt Foot Brown" as a result. Becoming a confirmed Loyalist, he vented his fury on the frontier families of the Parish. Stirring up the Creeks against the Rebels, raising a small army of Tories (Rangers), and accepting a King's commission as an officer to lead them, Brown made his persecutors pay in full with interest. The Creeks and their allies, already unhappy with white encroachment, welcomed his invitation to punish the settlers and did so.[11]

Indicative of the situation, one upcountry lad named James Cartledge was drafted into the Georgia Militia in February, 1778, spent six months in Florida and returned home later that year. Discharged, he immediately "went against the Indians as a volunteer who had committed depredations and murders upon the inhabitants (sic)." The situation became so bad, however, that he and other citizens had to flee to South Carolina for a time. Cartledge reentered the army, fought at Burke County Jail, January 26, 1779, and participated in the siege of Augusta. Later in the war, he was raised to captain and spent much effort repressing the Tories in the upcountry who were "increasing their depredations and cruelties and acted in small companies and mostly by night which required constant service to protect the inhabitants."[12]

The cruelty was not one-sided though. The Whigs could visit just as much suffering on innocent folks as the Tories. "In March of 1781, eleven of the Quakers (in Wrightsborough), most loyal to England, were murdered in their beds by a raiding party."[13] The fact that the Quakers were nonviolent, and conscientious objectors in any hostility, made them easy targets for the more radical of either side.

At Middleton's Ferry on the Savannah River in Columbia County, February 9, 1779, a skirmish was fought between a detachment of British under a Captain Whitney and Colonel Leonard Marbury's Patriot Dragoons from Brownsborough. The British had been sent to guard the crossing and were surprised by the Dragoons. Whitney and sixteen of his men were captured. After the Battle of Kettle Creek, in current Wilkes County, later that month, Marbury and his company were stationed at Brownsborough. Benjamin and William Few, Jr., with Silas Mercer as chaplain, served at the Battle of Burke County Jail, January 26, 1779. Few's brother, James, had been summarily hanged by supporters of the Crown in North Carolina, so the Fews, as a clan, were not kindly disposed toward the British. Many other upcountry men fought for the new nation also.

But life must go on locally as is said, and so it was in the communities of what became Columbia County. William Bartram meandered through the countryside to Augusta, apparently oblivious to the war around him.[14] William Few, Sr., while colonel of the district militia, was also appointed Justice of the Peace, June 20, 1776. His son, William Jr.. when he was not fighting in the war, attended the state general assemblies of 1777 and 1779. In the former, at Savannah, he was instrumental in forming the state constitution of 1777, which among other significant things, called for a courthouse and a jail for miscreants in every county in the state.

The 1777 Constitution did away with the parishes of Colonial times and instituted eight counties: Chatham, Glynn, Effingham, Richmond, Burke, Camden, Liberty and Wilkes.[15] The boundaries of some of these were very wide indeed, Richmond a major example. The first voting place, as mentioned, was Kiokee Meetinghouse in that same year. For the next six years, the voting was done in Brownsborough. Many of the citizens had to travel a long way for those days either from Wrightsborough or Augusta to vote. Nevertheless, when the war was over and attention could be properly turned to courthouses and jails, Few wanted the county seat in Brownsborough, In the 1780 General Assembly, he argued for that eventuality; the Assembly determined, however, that the "remote situation at Brownsborough rendered it a very unsafe place for a jail and courthouse." Few perhaps appreciated the irony of this statement—where would a better place be for a jail and courthouse than where lawlessness and vice made the area unsafe? At any rate, the Assembly tabled the matter.[16]

Few was undaunted. He and his friends of like mind, Abraham Baldwin, for instance, if they could not get the Richmond County seat in their area, then began to agitate for two county seats or better yet, a new county altogether. He sent letters to the Augusta Gazette such as the following which called for "...men who are in favor of a division of the county, that court buildings and trials may be erected and established..." At the urgent petitioning of Few and the citizens of the upcountry, the State Assembly on December 11, 1790, partitioned Richmond County in half and a new county was formed, named for Christopher Columbus, as recorded in the Augusta Chronicle And Gazette, February 26, 1791. If, as Ralph Waldo Emerson said, "An Institution is the lengthened shadow of one man," then William Few, Jr. is that man for Columbia County.

During the next few years, much happened in the new entity. In 1792, Columbia County was itself partitioned when the southwest corner was given to help form Warren County. On January 20, 1796, Governor Jared Irwin ordered militia districts and an organized militia. The county drew up 12 such districts (see appendix), formed a militia, and named William Few, Sr. as Colonel. For a humorous side of county militia drills, one may read Augustus Baldwin Longstreet's "The Militia Drill" in his Georgia Scenes.

During this time, veterans of the American Revolution were given land grants for their services. Elias Wilborn, for example, drew land in the county and became one of its wealthiest citizens. Edmund Cartledge drew a large estate. John Stapler was granted 350 acres on Euchee Creek, and Basil Neal drew many acres near Winfield which he named appropriately "Happy Valley." Human depravity being what it is, apparently there were also fraudulent claims made. In one case, twenty names were sent in in the same handwriting! "Among the worst offenders who thus acquired thousands of acres were Peter Carnes, Elijah Clarke, Leonard Marbury, Horatio Marbury, John Gorham, Edward Telfair, Ignatius Few..." Yet, much might be forgiven in a new world, the likes of which were never seen before:

> This was the first time in the history of the world, even the youngest boy knew that, in which the spirit of man had ever been quite untrammeled by despotism. ... Hope literally washed the heavens.[17]

It was heady wine for all, this new independence and nation, and the Columbia County people felt it as deeply as anyone. July 4th was a major celebration each year. They, however, began to move around in the area or westward where new lands were opening, so much so that some of the older communities began to empty out, especially Brownsborough. As the Assembly had said in 1780, the place was isolated and unsafe. Lawlessness was making life hard for peaceminded citizens. Restrictions on and punishment for crimes was desparately necessary. Out of this unrest grew the saga of the search for a suitable county seat. And saga it was!

William Few, Jr., who was out of the county much of the time, had wanted the county seat at Brownsborough. Since that town was so unsafe, he sought to make Kioka, the community which Daniel Marshall started, the seat. In the 1784 Assembly, Few had offered an amendment that the county seat be located "at the Little Kiokee on the new road which leads from Augusta to the Kiokee Meeting House where the said road crosses the Little Kiokee Creek." [18] This was before the county was created, so when the new county came to be, he apparently pushed to hold the local government business in Kioka. One source indeed says that the first courthouse was built there. [19]

But the mystery thickens, and reads like a latter-day soap opera filmscript. Adiel Sherwood wrote in 1827 that Cobbham was made the first "seat of justice" when the county was formed in 1790. [20] Construction was thus commenced and ran apace on the new jail and courthouse in Cobbham until on September 17, 1791, Augusta Chief Justice George Walton of the Supreme Court could state (Note: the following quotations are given in full, else no one would believe what transpired):

> The Commissioners of the Courthouse and jail at Cobb's Place, for the County of Columbia, having reported to us by their certificate dated 20th of August, last—that the Courthouse is sufficiently finished for business, and the Jail will be, before the sitting of the court. It is considered that the said courthouse, so finished, is the LEGAL place for holding the courts in and for the said County. [21]

If, as another source has it, Ignatius Few donated five acres for that structure, why does the good Justice call it Cobb's Place and why does Ignatius side against William? Whatever, with buildings

29

nearly complete at Cobbham, some citizens wanted the seat somewhere else. It seems that the "heady wine" of freedom was inebriating to the utmost! Justice Walton was not amused:

> The Grand Jury, taking into consideration the inconvenience sustained by the citizens from the itinerancy of the Courthouse and Jail, presents as a grievance that the late commissioners, after a new and well-built courthouse and jail had been erected and nearly completed, should have pointed out a different place for erecting such Publick Buildings, not more centrally located than the present. I would like to instruct them not to be swayed by malice or private "pique" in their judgements. William Stevens has completed his contract in building the Courthouse except for a table, and the upper windows made to open, for which deficiency we recommend that 40 shillings be deducted, unless the same are done before the next meeting of the Superior eourt. [22]

The citizens of the new county, perhaps because of the great distance which separated them from the agitated Judge, forged ahead. In February 1792, one William Appling sold some acreage for a mere pittance some miles from Cobbham for the express purpose of the seat of the county being there. This, to exacerbate matters, was also some four miles or so west of Kioka where, as mentioned, one source said a courthouse was located. Judge Walton, upon seeing this audacity which amounted to an insult upon his robes, could barely restrain his choler at his March 1792 sitting of the Superior Court. He refers almost contemptuously to the fluid state of the county seat as "itinerancy":

> This county, although it is now in separate creation, is a considerable fruition of one of the most ancient counties in the State. Many, or all of you are well conversant in the duties of your present Appointments; they are to present offences against the Laws for Public examination without regard for anything but truth. The spirit of Party which has been so prominent has made impressions of disagreements and produced consequences of much inconvenience. It is high time that they should give way to a more happy understanding. Had not the factions in the Fleet of

Columbus ceased as they did, you would not have the
honor of the name of the great discoverer of America
nominated for your county. I need not mention in
particular that I have in view the evils which have arose
from the itinerancy of your courthouse and jail. [23]

What the good Justice was saying in all that verbiage was that
the Columbia County commissioners were remiss in their duties
and needed to, as the saying goes, get their ducks in a row.

The ever-industrious citizens of the new county began
construction on a courthouse-jail complex in the village of
Applington without anyone's official permission and with attendant
squabbles about taxes levied to pay for it. So, now, there were two
courthouses and jails in the county, maybe three if one had indeed
been built at Kioka as mentioned above—a county, one should
remember, which had been formed expressly because Richmond
County had been too small for two county seats!

Finally, the General Assembly had to step in and settle the
matter. On November 29, 1794, it was resolved

That the seat of the public buildings in the county of
Columbia, as far as relates to the courthouse and jail
therein, shall be on that public lot of land, which was
conveyed by William Appling, to the commissioners of the
court-house and jail, it being the lot of land on which the
aforesaid buildings do now stand.[24]

The village of Applington (later Appling), however, was not
chartered until 1816. Another source says that the courthouse was
built in 1812. [25] This last could have been a new structure to
replace the one the Legislature said was already standing in 1794.
Applington then was a reality long before it was officially
chartered. Thus ended the saga of the courthouse odyssey in
Columbia County. Suffice it to say that by the time of the second
British invasion of 1812, Appling, from then onward, was the seat
of government for the county.

The various treaties with the Native Americans effectively moved them westward from the county and with them went many fears of further molestation of the white populace. The citizens settled down to peaceful pursuits of farming, mercantiling, blacksmithing, and, of course, politics. Eli Whitney's cotton gin, invented in 1793, had a spectacular effect on the preparation of that fiber for market and on the agriculture of the county. A county citizen named Jesse Bull also invented a gin.

> It may be, (wrote Dr. H.R. Casey) that the idea was suggested to each of these wise heads about the same time. Whitney brought action in the courts against Bull for infringement of his patent, Whitney offered him $10000 if he would allow judgement to be rendered against him; . . . (Bull) refused to be Bulldozed. [26]

Waverly Hall was the home of Dr. H.R. Casey, an eminent doctor of medicine and a delegate to the Georgia Secession Convention. Dr. Casey was a leader in politics before and after the Civil War. (Courtesy of Lallie Dozier Benkoski.)

The War of 1812, except for the fear of renegade Indians (which was almost pandemic in all parts of the United States, a national paranoia perhaps), did not disturb the County. There was no civil violence as had been with the Tories three decades earlier. Some of the men who served in the war were the five Hardin brothers. Stephen Drane also served under General Andrew Jackson, first as a lieutenant then a major. He subsequently became brigadier general of the militias of Richmond, Columbia, and Warren Counties. Later, he was major general of a six-county militia. Daniel Appling was a lieutenant in the regular army and defended a fleet of boats against a superior enemy on Lake Erie in 1812. He died in 1818 as a colonel. Appling's service in the war was applauded by the Georgia House, October 22, 1814; in honor of his exploits on Lake Erie, it resolved "that his Excellency, the Govenor, be, and he is hereby requested to have purchased and presented to him an elegant sword suitable for an officer of his grade." [27]

The county continued to grow in the early decades of the 1800's. The wilderness was cleared; several large plantations spread out around the villages as wealthy landowners turned to raising cotton and buying slaves. Cotton was in high demand on the national and export markets, but delivery was the great necessity for the growers. Flatboats on the Savannah River could carry the cargo, it was true, but a swifter means of transportation for goods and personal travel was needed. As Charles Ramsdell points out:

> The planter who went far into the interior found difficulty in getting his cotton to market. He must either wait upon a rise in the river and depend on occasional small steamers or the risky method of floating his crops down on rafts; or he must haul it during the wet winter season along nearly impassable roads.[28]

The advent of the railroad was one remedy. Visionaries were quick to point out that the ribbons of iron were the path of the future. "The coming of the railroads was of extreme importance;

on them awaited the rise and fall of cities, and the growth and decline of whole sections." [29] So it was with Columbia County. In 1833-36, the Georgia Railroad was laid between Augusta and Athens, running through the southern part of the county and leaving the vaster part of the county untouched. This would have a profound effect on the communities of the upper portion. In time, the county seat would become isolated. How tragically true! But that was later.

Local tradition has it that another railroad, the Augusta and Chattanooga, was projected through the county above Appling. On the properties of Joe Tankersley and Billy Snellings, evidences of old railroad grades are to be found which if charted on the map line up as surveyed. What became of this endeavor is not known, but such happened in other counties around the state where for whatever reason a company proposed to lay a railroad but could not get funds or else went into receivership.

In politics, George W. Crawford was elected to Governor of the state by the Whig party in 1843. During his two terms in office, the number of senators was reduced to forty-seven and representatives to one hundred and thirty. The debt of the state was decreased. During his tenure, the Mexican War came and eleven companies of soldiers and later two battalions were raised in the state. Some of Columbia County's youth volunteered and served in the hostilities. In the last year of his second term, Crawford advised the Senate in 1847 that in designing policies regarding slaves and other matters, one "cannot be too often and intently turned to Heaven for guidance and guardianship." [30] His advice was to have an ominous ring in the decade ahead.

The Jarrell plantation, the Woodville estate, Cedar Grove plantation, the McGruder estate, the David Harris plantation (which had the first frame house built in the county), the Cedarvale estate, and the Tubman plantation—all of these great farms and more flourished in the county. A lady who visited the county at this time wrote of the "broad piazzas where many-hued geraniums and broad-leafed coladiums grew in fancy pots and exquisite roses and brilliant annuals in the garden, making the scene an exquisite study in color," AUGUSTA CHRONICLE, October 29, 1987. By 1850, there were 3677 whites, 8272 slaves, and 72 free Negroes. Cotton was truly king. The railroad aided in the prosperity of the owners, for it provided the easiest and cheapest mode of delivering their product. To augment these huge farms, there were tanyards, gristmills, sawmills, barkmills, cotton gins and stores.

As a part of this prosperity, a new courthouse was built in Appling. Some miles from Appling, on the Savannah River, another innovation was built which, with the railroad, helped expedite shipping of goods to market. The Augusta Canal, which had been dug some years before, was opened November 23, 1846. The headgates and dam for this were in Columbia County. According to Michael White, AUGUSTA CHRONICLE, April 9, 2000, "Petersburg Boats and other water craft carrying produce and cotton from Columbia County farms to the markets of Augusta began using the canal transportation routes several months after the canal began flowing."

But the large plantations, which numbered twelve over 1000 acres in 1860, were not the only agricultural units in the county. There were smaller farms of 500 to 100 acres or less all over the area. Some of these farmers had one or two slaves, but most did not. Large or small, however, many planters and farmers shared one thing in common—a general misuse or abuse of the land.

> The general practice of the day was to exhaust and then abandon the soil. Red gullies and gulches were multiplying over the landscape. Unsightly undergrowths of briars and old-field pines were returning once fertile and productive fields to their primeval state.[31]

Such unscientific practices were to have woeful consequences for Columbia County in the following decades.

Some planters, however, were foresighted enough to use imagination in their husbandry of the soil. One of the planters in the county "did not run heavy on cotton . . . . He always had corn, wheat and oats for sale, and hence farming was a success with him and his large property increased under judicious management."[32]

The times were rosy indeed for the people of the county. "These were the halcyon days," remembered one, almost wistfully, ". . . days when money was handled as if it grew on trees." [33] It certainly was. The total value of personal property at that time was a felicitous $5,654,083 and real estate values were $1,925,083. The bubble was, however, ready to burst. Columbia County had a civilization which, if anyone had known, was about to disappear forever.

ON THE AUGUSTA
CANAL TOW-PATH.

Part II

War and Aftermath

In the 1860 census, there were 3567 whites, 8293 slaves and a few free Blacks who were virtually slaves with the legal restrictions which were put upon them. All, from least to the greatest, were aware of the tense political climate which had been heating up for the past decade over the issues of states' rights, economics, and the expansion of slavery into the territories which were opening up in the west. The Compromise of 1850 had been a tourniquet, which stopped the national bleeding for a time. But the tourniquet was being loosened by Abolitionists of the North who were calling for the removal of slavery and the radical element in the South who were agitating for, as Robert Toombs wrote to Alexander Stephens, "breaking up the concern (Union)."[34]

In addition to these national issues, another factor added to the foreboding of the time, the myth that the slaves really were content in their bondage, that Ole Massa was really taking good care of them. Nothing is further from the truth. Actually, "the slaves deeply resented their enslavement ... " writes James Oakes,

> Slaveholders complained that their bondsmen were impudent because they <u>were</u> impudent. Masters complained that their slaves were lazy because they frequently would

not work. By deliberate lassitude, by running away, by sabotage, slaves withheld their labor from the master.[35]

So then, the year of 1860 was a threshold over which the citizens of the nation would step into a cataclysm which would alter their destinies forever.

Politically, the state of Georgia had the Southern Rights Democrats who wanted John C. Breckinridge for president of the United States; the moderate Democrats who wanted Stephen Douglas for chief executive; and the Constitutional Unionists who wanted John Bell. The secession-minded Southern Rights Democrats, to no one's surprise, won in Georgia; nationally, Abraham Lincoln of the new Republican Party, of course, won it all. This was the last straw for the Southerners. Georgia Governor Joseph E. Brown called a state convention on November 21, 1860, and from that came the Secession Convention of January 16, 1861, in Milledgeville. Columbia County sent three delegates to the latter: Dr. H.R. Casey, physician-planter; Dr. W. A. Collins, physician-planter; and R.S. Neal, planter. George W. Crawford was elected Permanent President of the Convention and was escorted to his chair at the Convention by his good Whig friend, Alexander H. Stephens. After able arguments for and against the fateful move, the question was called; all three Columbia County delegates voted with the majority for secession. Convention President Crawford then announced it was "his privilege and pleasure to declare that the State of Georgia was free, sovereign, and independent."[36]

Secession was formally declared on January 19, 1861. "The action of the Secession Convention was acclaimed by general jubilation and celebration. There were bonfires, barbecues, and mass meetings to proclaim the advent of better days." Sitting in a trench around Petersburg, Virginia, in 1864, G.T. McCord, a young artilleryman from Columbia County, thought of these days in a letter to a friend:

38

It is pleasant recollection to let the mind revert back to the
past to the scene of youthful days and ponder over the
many pleasant moments of life but this reverie is brought to
an end by thinking how long will it be before those days
will be enacted again. But those days are gone never to
return.   Similar ones may come but under different
circumstances altogether. [37]

Young men like McCord flocked to join up for the army in
1861.It was another of those heady times.   The County filled at
least three companies of volunteer infantry for the Cause—
Thomson Guards, Company F, 10th Georgia Regiment; Ramsey
Volunteers, Company K, 16th Georgia Regiment; and Hamilton
Rangers, Company K, 48th Georgia Regiment. [38] The County
also gave two generals to the Cause: Henry Lewis Benning, who
became a major general, nicknamed "The Rock" for his tenacity in
battle; and James Clanton, who led Alabama troops in the Army
of Tennessee. [39]

As with any war in the nation's history, the young men went
away from home as boys and returned, if indeed they did come
back alive, as old men, with nothing in between. The horrors of
combat, the tedium of camp life, the ravages of disease, the
disfigurement of horrible wounds—all these forever changed the
survivors.   John C. Smith, who lived near Euchee Creek, sent
three of his sons to the war; none came back.   This pitiful
experience was repeated in other families as well.

Captain William Johnston of the Thomson Guards, while he
himself was in a hospital in Winchester, Virginia, perhaps
summed up the feelings of most if not all his fellow Georgians in a
letter to his wife, October 4, 1862:

Ruthless! Bloody War! the saddest of all evils—No grave
historian has ever written nor weeping poet sung its
dreadful ills. 'Tis writ in tears and blood—'Tis writ upon
the fields of strife where a man in deadly combat meets his
fellowman. 'Tis written there with glittering sword amid the
cannons roar, the clash of arms, 'Tis written upon the
ground strewn with the slain. 'Tis writ upon the mangled

bodies of the wounded all wet with their own gore—'Tis writ upon the midnight air made dismal-dismal-with the cries and groans of the dying—'Tis writ upon the stern solemn face of the warrior as he wraps up his comrade and lays him away in the cold earth far away from his home—'Tis writ upon the sad countenance of mothers, wives, and sisters whose homes and hearts have been made desolate. How many of the brave and good-the noble-have fallen!

Another county youth, G.T. McCord, an officer in the artillery, wrote to his "friend Nora," July 29, 1863:

Since I heard from you last I have seen and heard much. I went with the army when and where it went. Was at the battle of Gettysburg. ... Suffice it to say it was the hardest fought battle of the war. The heaviest cannonading ever known on the third. Gen. Lee says if all had have fought like the artillery those heights would have been captured. Our loss was very heavy ... [40]

In the war, the Thomson Guards lost 23 killed in action and 21 of disease, 34% of their total. The Ramsey Volunteers had 21 killed in battle and 22 of disease, 34%. The Hamilton Rangers lost 22 killed in combat, 28 of disease, 31 %. In all, the total of the county's youth who died in the war in these and other units was at least 154.

The home front during this trying period had its share of suffering, but of a different sort. The wife had to run the farm or plantation, look after the children, oversee the slaves, if any, bring out the old spinning wheel and loom to make clothing, and through it all worry about her dear one at the front. "She won no medals— did not want any, if the truth be known. She lived for the brief furloughs; she prayed for the quick end of hostilities; she dreamed of the return of her husband. For many women, the terse message from an officer or chaplain would announce the worst news of all."[41]

When the cotton bales started to pile up on the wharves of Confederate ports because of the blockade, and when it became painfully obvious that the Union was going to stay in the war for keeps, the Confederate government soon put limits on the growth of cotton with emphasis instead on the planting of food grains such as corn, wheat and oats. Cotton was limited to three acres per hand with a heavy fine for miscreants. Distilleries were curbed except for those of the government because they used grain which was needed for solid food. In 1862, 5,000,000 acres of Georgia land were planted in foodstuffs.

In most of the homes in the South, the lowly yam or sweet potato became "the staff of life in the war diet—roasted, baked, fried, boiled and even 'puddinged' for dessert."[42] When sugar became scarce, ribbon cane and sorghum were used. Salt, too, became almost impossible to procure even at the ridiculously high prices charged. Wives used ashes from the fireplace to cure bacon as the salt disappeared. They learned from the slaves that pork would cure very well packed in shucked corn on the cob.

If times were hard, though, for the white families, they were doubly so for the slaves, They had to do hard labor in the fields while subsisting (as the war went on) on short rations which finally became only molasses and bread. It even got tragically worse for the slaves in Columbia County. In 1862, hundreds of slaves died along the Savannah River for lack of food. "There the slaves could not even catch the fish abounding in the river because of the lack of fishhooks and lead weights for nets." A former slave on the

Jarrell Plantation stated that during the war, "… sometimes didn' have nothin' to eat but piece of cornbread…"[43]

Nothing, however, is so illustrative of the famine in Confederate Georgia and the county as the ingenious ways the people tried to substitute for the lack of coffee beans. Dried okra seed, sweet potatoes, corn meal, parched acorns, peanuts, and sorghum tops were all used for an ersatz coffee. How this brew must have tasted is a cause for pure wonderment!

To finance the war effort, the government issued bonds at various percentages of yield. People who could invested heavily in these with patriotic zeal, with high hopes of an ultimate Southern victory and a generous return on their investments. In some cases, people replaced all their United States money with Confederate bills, an ominous matter to be sure. Those who hoarded their U.S. greenbacks were the fortunate ones as matters turned out.

Even the churches felt the burden of the war. Kiokee Baptist for instance, as the chart shows, experienced a sharp decline in both white and black membership in 1863.[44] It is an interesting thing to notice on the chart that after 1863, to the end of the war two years later, the black membership began to rise steadily while the white rose much more slowly. In fact, the years 1861 and 1862 saw a "period of spiritual growth and increased religious activities." [45] Confederate victories of those years assured the people that God was indeed clothed in Rebel gray. But the disastrous setbacks at Vicksburg and Gettysburg in 1863, accompanied by horrendous casualties, had a ripple effect on the religious sensibilities of the people—Jehovah might be wearing Yankee blue after all.

Chart of black and white population from Kiokee Baptist
Church follows:

42

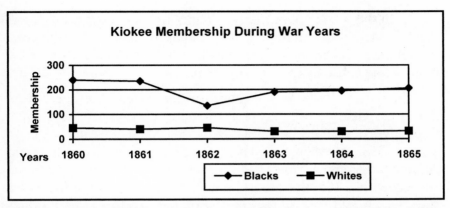

The Methodist denomination, which had records for charge conferences, annual conferences, and so forth, printed each year, revealed very well the climate of spirituality in its ranks. The Methodist churches in Columbia County were on a circuit, pastored by two ministers. In 1860, 423 white members and 366 black members were reported for that circuit. In 1861, 381 whites and no blacks were listed. In 1862, 348 whites and 382 blacks were present. In 1863, no whites and 430 blacks were counted. There was no report in 1864 for either. In 1865, reports at the end of the year had 441 whites and 260 blacks.[46]

The variables in both Baptist and Methodist churches in the county are as follows:

1. Obviously, many white laymen went to the war and took black servants with them.

2. Spirituality was measured by successes of the armies as in 1862, when victories came, churches prospered.

3. In the Methodist church, reports were not turned in at times for whatever reason.

4. It was difficult for the Methodist bishop to have annual conferences or to fill pulpits. George Foster Pierce for example wrote a friend, October 21, 1861: "The war has cut me off from all my conferences."

5. In the Columbia County Circuit, in 1865, there were fewer blacks, for that denomination was seeing an exodus of ex-slaves. All religious denominations in the state were seriously affected by the war and subsequent reconstruction.

The county, in the late war, also saw an influx of refugees from northwest Georgia who were fleeing the ravages of the Atlanta Campaign of 1864, Later that year, many others came in from central Georgia when Sherman began his notorious march from Atlanta to Savannah which cut the heart out of the state. When the war ended in 1865, the county reflected the condition of the entire state which had lost "three-fourths of her wealth. Land values decreased by one-fourth and the slaves, valued at $454,042,282, in 1860 were a total loss."[47] Columbia County with its huge plantations and hundreds of slaves, suffered in precise proportion to the state: true farm values were listed at $1,136,235, a decrease of 41% of that reported in the 1860 census.

The condition of one of these planters is indicative of them all:

> The late war and its long train of evil, the loss of his slave property, depreciation of lands, scarcity of money and heavy percent for advances, have told greatly on his surrounds, and today the labor on his farm of only a few acres is done by himself and his three sons.[48]

This particular planter had owned two large estates before the war. But overall, it was bad: "Farming implements and stock had been taken or destroyed, plantations were overgrown with weeds, . . . Bad cotton seed, 4 or 5 years old, came up about one in a thousand." One traveler through the county in 1866 wrote:

> Rail-fences, old and delapidated buildings, and rough cultivation, greeted your eye constantly; relieved only by great numbers of majestic trees, and occasionally by the sight of a fine mansion some distance from the road. [49]

On August 6, 1865, Paul Hamilton Hayne wrote to his wife from Augusta: "Thus far, I have escaped the taking of the Oath. It is sad to observe how thoroughly our People have been conquered. As for Editors (he was an editor at the time on the <u>Augusta Constitutionalist</u>), they occupy the tightest of straight jackets." [50] Hayne had left Charleston after the Federals burned his home and magnificent library and would soon build a cottage at the railway station which would become Grovetown. In his comment to his wife, he alluded to two things that were going to be symptomatic of the next decade in the South: The people were absolutely conquered and near destitution; and the Federal authorities scrutinized everything, especially newspapers. The Oath he mentioned was the Oath of Allegiance to the United States.

Those persons who had purchased heavily in Confederate and Georgia bonds lost everything in the end. In October 1865, the state treasury had $5,706,500 in cash on hand, but this amount was illusory at best since only $44,750 was in U.S. specie. [51] So, bonds bought during the late "unpleasantness" to underwrite Georgia's participation in the abortive nation could not be paid except in Confederate money which, needless to say, was absolutely and utterly worthless, except maybe for the price of the paper it had been lithographed on. The planter after the war then had to borrow money for seed, food, and other necessities at interest rates in some areas at 2 percent per month, with a US tax of 2 ½ cents on every pound of cotton , according to the <u>Augusta Chronicle</u>, May 13, 1866.

The Negro, who had been the labor force in slavery, was still at the bottom of the socioeconomic scale; maybe more so now, for in slavery he was at least worth something as chattels. Now, he was on his own, with a family to feed and an overweening white supremacy philosophy on the part of those in power, North and South, to deal with. Many of them remained on the estates they had worked on before the war, earning a small wage for their work. "The very danger feared by all whites throughout the South had come to pass... the slave had become a free laborer, and he must be taken care of."[52] The last phrase here had an ominous ring to it, for with everything taken away from them, the whites looked on the Negro as a Sambo, the lowest one could get on the scale of society. He became the scapegoat for the ills of the state.

But many of the freed persons were determined to make their way in life regardless. Two men for example advertised in the <u>Augusta Chronicle</u>, January 31, 1866:

> We are prepared to do all manner of wood and iron work—wagon making and repairing included. We have not turned fools because we are free, but know we have to work for our living, and are determined to do it. We mean to be sober, industrious, honest, and respectful to white folks, and so we depend on them to give us work (signed) William and Jim.

Many of the white planters were sincere in their wanting to help the Negro. This sincerity stemmed from two motivations, the lesser perhaps being plain humaneness, the other from the need for labor on the farms. The laborer was paid either in cash or in shares of the crops. "Where money was paid," stated S.M. Mays of Columbia County in 1915, "it was common practice to pay one half at the end of each month and the other half at the end of the year. This was done to hold the Negro, if possible, until the the end of harvest season." Some of the freedmen struck out on their own and did very well. Charles Stearns was approached by one who wanted to rent 20 acres so he could farm independently of the sharecropping system. Stearns rented him the land and the ex-slave grew three times more cotton than Stearns' sharecroppers on the same amount of acreage![53] But the number of hands employed decreased from 2789 in 1867 to 1090 in 1872.[54]

To make matters worse in the next few years, racial unrest was rife in the county. The local government was controlled by the Negroes who as before outnumbered the whites by a large margin. The leader was Romulus Moore, born in the county in 1813, a mulatto, who had bought his freedom before the war. He was a blacksmith, a Baptist minister, and a boardinghouse keeper. Listed in the 1870 census as literate, he had a personal wealth of $1300.00. The Freedman's Bureau hired him to register the freedmen in the county to vote. A Republican, he was elected to the Georgia House in 1866-1868. Moore tried to be amicable to the whites and fair in his dealings with them. Nevertheless, election days at Appling were not pretty scenes, but truth is and truth must be told. The following affidavit is illustrative of the white peoples' reaction to Republican voters, especially freedmen:

> Willis Jackson; lives on C. Stearns's place, Columbia County, Georgia; was at the election at Apling (sic), December 20 (1870), and saw a white man strike Charles Harding over the head with a hickory stick of the size of a common broom-handle, because Harding said he voted the radical ticket. About the same time another white man kicked my father, Eli Jackson, because he said he had voted the radical (Republican) ticket. In my opinion over five hundred colored people were, on that day, prevented from voting. The white people were going about, drawing their pistols, and cutting at the colored people who attempted to vote the radical ticket, and threatening to kill them if they thus voted. (signed) Willis Jackson. [55]

The problem was exacerbated, by the presence of the hated "carpetbagger," the Northerner or, worse, the Southerner or "scalawag" who ostensibly was there to help the ex-slave adjust to freedom. Most of their work, though, was for self-aggrandisement. They were hated by the whites, and, of course, the Negro was caught in the middle. There were several instances of black-on-white or white-on-black crimes, as well as what were termed "outrages." In March, 1868, a klavern of the Ku Klux Klan was organized in Augusta with units in surrounding counties. On March 31 of that year, the AUGUSTA CHRONICLE carried an editorial which was a not-too-thinly-veiled warning to "traitors, scalawags, and bummers."

In the lower part of the county, the unit there was inactive, but in the upper part, where the county seat was located, there was much more unrest; the Klan, in July 1869, "forcibly removed from jail and put to death a freedman and his wife, accused of murder," according to the <u>Macon Telegraph</u>, August 11, 1869. The perpetrators, to no one's great surprise, were never found. To illustrate the fear of the Klan among Republicans in the county (which included most of the Negroes), one need only see the figures for the election of 1868: 1222 blacks voted for Republican, Rufus Bullock, in the gubernatorial election in April, 1868; when in November the presidential question was on the ballot, only 1 black voted for U.S. Grant. The intimidation was obviously working. [56] The work of the Klan, then, instilled a sense of dread, disdain, and deep suspicion of the white man, which after 125 years still has not been expunged, if ameliorated somewhat.

On August 26, 1868, the Georgia House expelled all persons of color.[57] Romulus Moore was the Columbia County representative to be thus ousted; he and the others were subsequently reinstated. Indeed, he had been visited by a committee of Klansmen and was told, "You think that you negroes and radicals are going to control this country, but white men in the North, the aristocracy of the North, have always controlled the poorer classes of people, and we intend to do it here." He summed up the plight of the Negro quite well in the February 1, 1871, meeting of the State Commission of Colored Men in Atlanta: Blacks could not receive justice in Georgia and should emigrate to the Promised Land which was, unaccountably, Arkansas. [58]

When the period of Reconstruction was finally declared over in 1872, not much had been reconstructed. The Negro, who had been promised much by the Freedman's Bureau, found himself socially and economically no better off than he had been as a slave. Now, he had to try to make a living while depending on the very people who had been his masters and who were at this point in time very hostile. The Freedman's Bureau realized finally that the violence of the whites against its policies and plans had annulled its work, that when the army was withdrawn, the black man would be utterly alone:

> In August 1868, Lieutenant H. Catley, the Bureau's officer
> in Augusta, expressed his belief that without the presence
> of the federal government, 'the condition of the blacks will

48

be even worse than when in slavery.' ... Planters were already scheming to keep down the price of labor while warning their employees to expect stern treatment now that the Bureau 'is run out.' [59]

They certainly were worse off. The enmity between the races did not lessen perceptibly with the passage of time. The white citizenry, on the other hand, regained power in the County until one of them could boast in the <u>Columbia County Sentinel</u> in 1883:

> ... she (the county) did not permit this political fraud to stain her bright escutcheon but for a short time, when rising in her might she soon calmed the storm of Radicalism and put her own intelligent and honest citizens in power.

The writer of this "boast," an eminent county physician who had been a delegate to the Secession Convention in 1861, is the same one who tried to prevent the Negroes from voting the Republican ticket in 1870:

> The doctor, by threats and show of weapons, prevented the colored men from crossing the bridge (at Appling) until the lieutenant came with his men, crossed the bridge, and took possession of the guns, placed a guard over them, relieving some twenty-five colored men from their charge. [60]

Agriculturally, during the post-war years, cotton was still grown for the cash markets, with little thought for conservation of the soil. This, coupled with periodic droughts, a depression in the 1870's, and the creation of McDuffie County from the western half of Columbia County in 1871 was to have a lasting effect for the county. In 1872, however, a national movement for agricultural reform named "The Grange" was started. At Bethel Baptist Church in the county, a local chapter of the Grange, as it was called, was set up. Local farmers, as elsewhere after the war, were disorganized and discouraged, The Grange was designed to bring the farmers together. "They operated crop reporting services, organized community social activities, managed co-operative buying and selling exchanges, sponsored experience meetings

..."[61]   The Farmers' Alliance also sought answers for the agricultural dilemma facing not only the county but the nation as well. However, between 1870 and 1900, "The value of the average farm (including implements, machinery, and stock) dropped from $1,849 to $1,016 ..."[62]   Still the county held its first agricultural fair in Harlem in 1890.

An unidentified 1839 plantation home. The photo was taken c. 1940. (Courtesy of G.L. Polatty.)

As the railroads recovered from the ravages of the Civil War, Harlem and Grovetown began to grow as important railroad stops. They took on aspects of significant and popular resort areas for the people of Augusta. In 1892, the Charleston and Western Railroad laid tracks through the northeastern part of the county. One depot was named Jenkins for the donor of the right of way, Mrs. Sarah Jenkins. A few miles away, another depot was built and named Evans for Confederate General George Washington Evans, not Clement Evans. No hard evidence has been found to indicate that the town was named for the famous Confederate general, author, and Methodist minister, Clement Anselm Evans. The Jenkins stop later became the village of Martinez; the second Evans.

In the Spanish-American War of 1898,"Georgians almost forgot the Civil War, as the flag took on a glow which it had not shed since 1861 .. ." [63] Perhaps the war outside the country took the minds of the people off their troubles. At least three of the county's youth served in Cuba.

At the turn of the century, the county was still basically agrarian, O.B. Stevens reported:

> The soil of two-thirds of the land is red clay. In the pinelands of the southern part of the county the soil is sandy with clay subsoil. On the river the lands are fertile and produce good crops of cotton, corn, sugar-cane, potatoes, melons and peas. Though some of the lands are much worn with bad tillage, intelligent cultivation is in many places restoring its fertility. ... About 3,000 acres are devoted to raising melons for the market, the net profit on which is about $25 an acre. ... the cotton ginned for the season of 1899-1900 was 9,354 bales of upland. [64]

Tom Watson's Populist stance helped the farmers also. In all truth, they needed help, as the Columbia Sentinel stated in 1908: "Cool nights, cotton looks sick, gardens unusually poor, eggs and chickens scarce, beef a thing of the past ..." A county native, there was much in Watson's words about the poor white and black man of the soil:

> You are kept apart that you may be separately fleeced of your earnings. You are made to hate each other because upon that hatred is rested the keystone of the arch of financial despotism which enslaves you both. [65]

Aside from the fact that the source of the hatred was somewhere else, Watson's words have a ring of truth about them. He was also at loggerheads with President Woodrow Wilson's policies, so World War I was not popular in the county.

Nevertheless, many of the county's youth went overseas, and at least four died in the trenches in 1918.

The promise of electricity for lighting came when the Stevens Creek Dam project was started in 1914; but the greatest invasion of the state since Sherman threatened the county with disaster was on its way: In 1915, the lowly boll weevil moved in and settled down in the cotton fields. For the next five years, it destroyed the cotton crops and left many of the county's farmers in extremis.

The non-farmers, those in the towns of the county, were having a better time of it, according to the <u>Columbia News</u>, November 1924:

> Columbia and vicinity is now enjoying a period of unprecedented prosperity and onward progress. Excellent public highways make motoring a pleasant pastime, homes are modern and well kept, the public utilities offer the best of service, the churches and schools are of the best in the country.

If some of these people had "motored" out into the county, they might have seen something akin to what Erskine Caldwell saw in a nearby county:

> Day after day I went into the county, becoming more depressed by what I saw as I traveled farther and farther from settlements and highways. I could not become accustomed to the sight of children's stomachs bloated from hunger and seeing the ill and aged too weak to walk to the fields to search for something to eat. [66]

The 1929 crash ushered in the Great Depression years. Banks closed or failed everywhere; money was scarce. The old barter-for-goods returned. During this time, unfortunate city-dwellers, set adrift from economic necessity, came into the county and occupied vacant houses left by those who had departed from the ravages of the boll weevil. [67] This period had a profound effect on the Negro population of the county, many of whom left for the North and its industries. In 1900, the county had 10,753 Negroes; by 1930, they numbered 5,536.

A writer for the <u>Augusta Chronicle,</u> October 19, 1930, lamented about the county, "there is now a desolation all around and the sadness of change is everywhere evident." The effects of the Depression were slow in retreating, as the following letter to Mrs. Eleanor Roosevelt from a young girl in Thomson revealed:

> I am a high school girl and I am in badly in need of clothes. ... if you have any that you will not need anymore I would certainly be glad to get them. It is imbarising the way I have to dress. ... I am 18 years of age weight about 127 lbs.—brown hair and grey eyes, No. 6 shoes.[68]

The conditions in the county were alleviated to a large extent by the programs inaugurated by President Franklin Roosevelt. The Rural Electrification Act finally lit some of the county's homes with electricity. The New Deal helped the county recover so much that it was honored as the most progressive in the state. Works Projects Administration funds built offices in Appling for court officials. The jail across from the courthouse was a product of the government's funds. The <u>Columbia News</u>, March 7, 1935, praised the new lock-up with its heat, baths, and other conveniences—one wonders how poor the other one was! But alas, there were no occupants:

> Now no prisoners are in sight, and the building is only used as a habitation for the jailers. However, the situation is not new, for Columbia County has been virtually prisonerless for the past three or four years.

Shades of Mayberry, North Carolina! But this problem of no inmates was destined to change phenomenally in the next five decades. In all candor, the reason the jail was empty was that the prisoners were most probably out on the notorious chain-gangs which were used to make "excellent public highways" mentioned above:

> ... accounts of the chain gang from the 1920's, 1930's and even late 1940's reveal that convicts continued to labor, eat, and sleep with chains riveted around their ankles. Work was done under the gun from sunup to sundown, shoveling dirt at fourteen shovelfuls a minute. Food was bug infested, rotten, and unvarying; rest was taken in unwashed bedding ... [69]

World War II brought economic relief to the county with the building of the Fort Gordon reservation in 1941 which incorporated some of the county's acreage. Many civilians were employed by civil service in the war effort. The county's forests underwent a severe harvest of walnut trees to make rifle stocks, from which the forests have not fully recovered. Sadly, of the many young men who served in the armed forces, fourteen paid "the last full measure" on the battlefields of Europe and in the Pacific theater.

The Savannah River Site nuclear facility which came in the 1950's brought with it thousands of employees, many of whom bought homes in the county. Interstate 20, which made distance of no consequence, abetted this situation. "Essentially, Columbia County grew as a 'bedroom area' of Augusta and Richmond County. That is, the county developed as a residential and service area of the city of Augusta," as one report stated. [70] The county grew very fast in the decades that followed. Too fast, indeed, because the influx of newcomers was taxing the resources of the county which for over a century had seen nothing like it.

The COLUMBIA NEWS reported, June 18, 1964, that the county was encountering severe sewerage problems:

> Health authorities have stated that the Martinez-Evans area is fast reaching a point where the building of more septic tanks will create a health hazard. ... Both the FHA and the Veteran's Administration ... say they will soon refuse to

lend money on housing to build in the vicinity if septic
tanks are used.

There were still several large farms in the southern part of the
county in the 1950's and 60's. The Webster farm, the Hereford
Farm, and the Sears, Roebuck farm—all were very large with
cows, food grains or chickens. These, however, were on acreage
soon largely consumed by urbanism. In fact, Martinez and Evans
as villages virtually disappeared in a maze of suburbs; the
upcountry around Appling remained much as it was before the turn
of the century.

Under the Flood Control Act of 1944, the Clark Hill Dam,
promised in 1926, was begun in 1946 and finished in 1950. The
reservoir thus begun on the Savannah River created the great
78,700 acre lake which now draws thousands to its recreational
facilities and parks (six million in 1995 alone). The wildlife
preserve that it offers is one of the best anywhere. On December
22, 1987, Public Law 100-209 changed the lake's name to Strom
Thurmond Lake, much to the chagrin of Columbia Countians.

A new government complex has been built in Evans; a new
courthouse is under construction; and an Evans Town Center is in
the making. Appling will feel this change acutely. A new library
is also projected. As Jason Smith stated in the Augusta Chronicle,
June 19, 2000:

> Five decades ago when most of Columbia County's roads
> were dirt and the 9,525 residents called such places as
> Winfield, Leah, and Berzelia home, a sense of community
> wasn't hard to find. Now as the county's population edges
> toward 100,000, it's up to the people who live there to
> shape and develop an identity that is beyond just being a
> suburb.

Chapter Two Footnotes

[1] E. Merton Coulter, Georgia A Short History (Chapel Hill: University of North Carolina Press, 1947), 102.

[2] Coulter, 62. See also Edward Cashin, "The Gentlemen of Augusta," Colonial Augusta: "Key Of The Indian Country" (Macon: Mercer University Press, 1986), 29-57.

[3] Dispatch from Governor James Wright, November 18, 1766, Shelburne Papers, 52:200 (Clements Library, Ann Arbor, Michigan).

[4] Allen Candler, ed. Colonial Records Of Georgia 10 (Atlanta: Franklin-Turner, 1914), 814-816.

[5] Robert Davis, Jr., Quaker Records In Georgia: Wrightsborough 1772-1793 And Friendsborough 1771-1777 (Roswell: Wolfe, 1986), 3-4, There are several popular history accounts about Brandon, but none are substantiated.

[6] Davis, 5.

[7] Letter to Reverend Thomas Percy, January 13, 1776 (Clements Library, Ann Arbor, Michigan). William Bartram described the upcountry just below Little River in 1773: "The face of the country is chiefly a plain of high forests, savannas and cane swamps." Edward Cashin,Ed., A Wilderness Still The Cradle Of Nature: Frontier Georgia (Savannah: Beehive, 1994), 45.

[8] Adiel Sherwood, Gazateer Of The State Of Georgia (Atlanta: Richards, 1829), 149. When graves were excavated in September 2000 at Milton Reuben Chevrolet, on the site of the old Quaker Springs, a slate tombstone was found with the date "1816" etched thereon, proving that a settlement was there.

[9] Waldo Harris III and James D. Mosteller, Georgia's First Continuing Baptist Church (Appling, Georgia: Kiokee Baptist Church, 1997), 19.

[10] Harris and Mosteller, 274-275.

[11] Edward Cashin, The King's Ranger (Athens, GA: University of Georgia Press. 1989), 21-30. It is interesting to point out here that almost a full year before the attack on Brown, Daniel Marshall, William Few and others, 83 in all, met at Tondee's Tavern in Savannah, August 10, 1774, and signed a document of dissent to the hotheaded radicalism of the Liberty Boys. The signees wanted time for deliberation before going to arms against Breat Britain; "We, the inhabitants of Kyokee and Broad River settlements, do in this public manner think proper to declare our dissent ..." George White, Historical Collections Of Georgia (New York: Pudney and Russell, 1854), 605-606. After the attack on Brown and other outrages by the Sons of Liberty, the signees had to get off the fence, so to speak, and most sided with the Revolutionary faction, particularly William Few, whose brother had been murdered by the British in 1771.

[12] National Archives and Records Administration, General Reference Branch, Washington, D.C., Pension Claim S.8167.

[13] Ralph Scott, Jr., "The Quaker Settlement of Wrightsborough," Georgia Historical Quarterly LVI (1972), 220. One must consider that as much as one-third of the Georgia population sided with good King George III during the Revolution. Those "Tories" lost everything after the war. See Heard Robertson, Loyalism In Revolutionary Georgia (Atlanta: Georgia Commission for the National Bicentennial Celebration and Georgia Department of Education, 1978) for a good discussion of this phenomenon.

[14] Cashin, A Wilderness Still In The Cradle, 45.

[15] Coulter, 150-151.

[16] <u>Revolutionary Records Of Georgia III</u> (Atlanta: Franklin-Turner, 1908) 422, 565-567. Also, George R. Lamplugh, "William Few's Brownsborough Plan," <u>Richmond County History 5</u> (Winter 1973), 40-45. It was dangerous in all truth. "If one traveled any distance from a settlement in 1785, there was the constant threat of encountering predatory creatures of both the two-legged and four-legged kind," George Lamplugh, "Farewell to the Revolution: Georgia in 1785," <u>Georgia Historical Quarterly LVI</u> (Fall 1972), 388.

[17] Alex Hitz, "Georgia Bounty Grants," <u>Georgia Historical Quarterly 38</u> (1954), 324. John Donald Wade, <u>Augustus Baldwin Longstreet: A Study Of The Development Of Culture In The South</u> (New York: Macmillan, 1924), 16.

[18] <u>Revolutionary Records Of Georgia III</u>, 555-567.

[19] Margaret Rodgers, <u>Historical Landmarks And Legends Of Columbia County</u> (Appling, GA: Historical Society, 1976), 11.

[20] Sherwood, 1830.

[21] Superior Court Records, Richmond County, 1791.

[22] Superior Court Records, Richmond County, 1791.

[23] Superior Court Records, Richmond County, 1792.

[24] <u>Revolutionary Records Of Georgia</u>.

[25] <u>Georgia Courthouse Manual</u> (Atlanta: Georgia Department of Community Affairs, 1992), 70.

[26] "Reminiscences of Dr. H.R. Casey," <u>Columbia County Sentinel</u>, September 13, 1883. Dr. Casey was a delegate to the 1850 Democratic Convention and to the Georgia Secession Convention in 1861. He was a close friend of Alexander H. Stephens.

[27] <u>Columbia Sentinel</u>, March 7, 1883. Northern, W.J. <u>Men Of Mark In Georgia, II,</u> (Atlanta: Caldwell, 1910), 55.

[28] Charles Ramsdell, "The Natural Limits of Slave Expansion," Mississippi Valley Historical Review 16 (1929), 151-171.

[29] Coulter, 258.

[30] Journal Of The Senate 1848, 210.

[31] Willard Range, A Century Of Georgia Agriculture (Athens: University of Georgia Press, 1954), 18. "Those Georgians who had advocated agricultural reform had long warned that soil-wrecking and inattention to food production could bring about a crisis. ... Three wretched harvests (1850's) drew a chorus of disappointment. 'The scarcity of Corn and Bread in some parts of Georgia is now beginning to create serious alarm' ... " George B. Crawford, "Cotton, Land, and Sustenance: Toward the Limits of Abundance in Late Antebellum Georgia," Georgia Historical Quarterly, Lxii (Summer 1988), 243.

[32] Columbia Sentinel, April 25, 1883.

[33] Columbia Sentinel, June 21, 1883.

[34] U.B. Philips, Ed. The Correspondence Of Robert Toombs, Alexander H, Stephens, And Howell Cobb II (Washington, D.C.: Government Printing Office, 1913), 449-450.

[35] The Ruling Race: A History Of American Slaveholders (New York:Vintage, 1983), 179.

[36] Journal Of The Convention At Milledgeville And Savannah 1861 (Milledgeville: Boughton, Nisbet and Barnes, 1861), 37-39

[37] T. Conn Bryan, Confederate Georgia (Athens: University of Georgia Press, 1953), 10. G.T. McCord to "Friend Nora," October 3, 1864, courtesy of the Dan Marshall Collection.

[38] Lillian Henderson, Ed. Roster Of The Confederate Soldiers Of Georgia (Hapeville, Georgia: Longino and Porter, 1956-1960), II & III, various pages.

[39] William C. Davis, Ed. <u>The Confederate Generals 4</u>, (Harrisburg: The National Historical Society, 1991) 50, 194.

[40] Thomas Holley, <u>Company F Thomson Guards Tenth Regiment Georgia Volunteers Army Of Northern Virginia Confederate States Of America</u> (Fernandina Beach, Florida: Wolfe, 2000), 305-306. See William C. Blackard, Thomas Huckabee, and Gerald J. Smith, <u>Columbia County, Georgia</u> (Charleston: Arcadia Press, 2000), for a photograph of Captain Johnston. G.T. McCord to "Friend Nora," July 29, 1863, courtesy of the Dan Marshall Collection.

[41] Gerald J. Smith, <u>Letters, Diaries And Reminiscences Of The Union And The Confederacy</u> (Murfreesboro, Tennessee: Ambassador, 1995), 84.

[42] Range, 43. <u>The American Slave: A Composite Autobiography</u> 12 (Westport, Connecticut: Greenwood, 1972), 114.

[43] Range, 48. <u>The American Slave: A Composite Autobiography</u> 12 (Westport, Connecticut: Greenwood, 1972), 114.

[44] Harris and Mosteller, 160.

[45] Bryan, 237.

[46] <u>Minutes Of The Annual Conferences Of The Methodist Episcopal Church, South</u> 1858-1865 II (Nashville: Southern Methodist Publishing House, 1859-1866), various pages.

[47] Bryan, 65.

[48] <u>Columbia Sentinel</u>, May 17, 1883.

[49] Mildred Thompson, <u>Reconstruction In Georgia</u> (Atlanta: Cherokee, 1971), 84. Charles Stearns, <u>The Black Man Of The South, And The Rebels: Or, The Characteristics Of The Former, And The Recent Outrages Of The Latter</u> (New York: American News Company, 1872), 34.

[50] Rayburn Moore, <u>A Man Of Letters In The Nineteenth Century South: Selected Letters Of Paul Hamilton Hayne</u> (Baton Rouge: Louisiana State University Press, 1982), 58.

[51] Bryan, 65.

[52] Coulter, 349.

[53] Thompson, 76. Stearns, 517.

[54] <u>Report Of The Comptroller General 1872</u> (Atlanta: Harrison, 1873), 322.

[55] Edmund Drago, "Georgia's First Black Voter Registrars during Reconstruction," <u>Georgia Historical Quarterly 78</u> (Winter 1994), 792. Strearns, 292-93.

[56] Thompson, 376. For a contemporary view of the KKK, see Stearns, 420-443.

[57] <u>Acts And Resolutions Of The General Assembly</u>, 1868, 222.

[58] Russell Duncan, <u>Freedom's Shore: Tunis Campbell And The Georgia Freedmen</u> (Athens: University of Georgia Press, 1986), 73. Edmund Drago, <u>Black Politicians And Reconstruction In Georgia: A Splendid Failure</u> (Baton rouge: LSU Press, 1982), 152.

[59] Paul Cimbala, "On the Front Line of Freedom: Freedmen's Bureau Officers and Agents in Reconstruction Georgia," <u>Georgia Historical Quarterly 76</u> (Fall 1992), 610-611.

[60] Stearns, 297.

[61] Range, 138.

[62] Range, 151.

[63] Coulter, 429.

[64] OB Stevens, <u>Georgia: Historical And Industrial</u> (Atlanta: Harrison, 1901), 612.

[65] Idus Newby, <u>The South A History</u> (New York: Holt, Rinehart, 1978), 338. This is the same Tom Watson who also "proposed that the Negro be eliminated from Georgia politics by 'a change in our Constitution which will perpetuate white supremacy in Georgia,' " Charlton Moseley, "Latent Klanism in Georgia 1890-1915," <u>Georgia Historical Quarterly LVI</u> (Fall 1972), 369.

[66] Richard Harwell, "Erskine Caldwell Georgia Cracker World-class," <u>The Atlanta Historical Journal 26</u> (Winter 1982-83), 12.

[67] Coulter, 432.

[68] Robert Cohen, "Public Schools in Hard Times: Letters to Eleanor and Franklin Delano Roosevelt, 1933-1942," <u>Georgia Historical Quarterly 72</u> (Spring 1998), 121-150.

[69] Alex Lichtenstein, "Good Roads and Chain Gangs in the Progressive South: "The Negro Convict is a Slave,'" The Journal of Southern History 59 (February 1983), 85.

[70] <u>Harlem's Community Development Plan</u> (Atlanta: Department of Community Development, 1977), 1.8.

—Chapter Three—

$\mathscr{E}$ducation

LEAH CONSOLIDATED SCHOOL
OPENED 1911-CLOSED 1956
PRINCIPAL MR.HATCHER HOGAN

As the settlers moved into the county, they brought with them their children and realized, as good parents, that the youth needed instruction. For a time, that teaching came at the fire hearth with the students learning to read and write through Bible catechism. The parents—the educated—also probably had a copy of Pilgrim's Progress and Shakespeare's Plays; though, be it added, these two did not usually appear on the same shelf! Some parents probably had some of the Classics. In other words, early on, education was a family matter.

The Georgia Constitution of 1777 was friendly toward local education, but it was the State Constitution of 1783, July 31, that called for academies in the counties, as well as "free schools."[1] These academies were ostensibly secondary schools and the free schools were to be elementary. The Constitution of 1798 was more specific: there were to be "arts and sciences in one or more seminaries of learning ..."[2]

On November 29, 1794, the Georgia Assembly, in the same act which placed the county seat in Applington, stated: "And be it further enacted, That the seat of the academy shall be at such place as the commissioners of the Columbia Academy or a majority of them shall deem proper ..."[3] But, the fly in the buttermilk, so to speak, was that there was no academy built at that time, nor one projected, for Applington.

One man, however, did have an academy in the county, one of the truly great educators in the state's history—Moses Waddel (pronounced "Waddle"). He, according to an advertisement in the <u>Southern Sentinel And Gazette Of The State</u>, January 9, 1794, established the school in Carmel, Georgia, on the "Kiokas" two miles or so from the county seat. The name, Kiokas, being plural, perhaps referred to the fork made where Greenbrier Creek joins Big Kiokee Creek, an area already settled with roads nearby. The site of Carmel, or Mt. Carmel, would then have been halfway between Kioka and Applington. Local tradition places his academy and church on Little Kiokee Creek near Appling. But what happened to the community, for no known map shows a Carmel village in the area? Waddel, a Presbyterian minister, came there in the first place to minister to his first charge, Mt· Carmel Presbyterian Church. Was there a Presbyterian meetinghouse on Greenbrier Creek?

Waddel refers to his academy as Carmel Academy for two years or so, but changed the name to Columbia Academy in order, speculated E. Merton Coulter, to get state funds. W.J. Northern indeed stated that after two years at Carmel, Waddel moved his school to Applington. Abraham Baldwin, one of the commissioners for the county academy, probably persuaded Waddel, who already had a school, that it would be in his best interests if it were removed to the county seat and renamed Columbia Academy.[4]

His school was a classical one, with rigid discipline and instruction in the Classics. He himself had been schooled in "the study of Latin and Greek languages, Euclid's Elements of Geometry, Moral Philosophy and Criticism,"[5] Illustrative is the following letter Waddel wrote to a father of one of his charges. Note the emphasis on the Classics and Waddel's deep concern for his students:

Columbia Academy
15th Dec.1798

Dear sir,

I have the pleasure of being able to inform you that your son & master Campbell are both well at present. They have improved considerably in Latin since you left them here; being now within a week's time of finishing Virgil. I most earnestly wish you would send them a Latin dictionary, a Greek Grammar, a Greek Lexicon. As they will finish Virgil before Christmas; I wish them to enter Cicero ~ the Greek Grammar immediately after the Academy commences at New Year's day. I am partly obliged to give a few days vacation at Christmas as a large number of the students wish to go home then for to see their connexions. If you can avail yourself of no other mode of conveyance, I recommend to send the books by the stage—the freight will be a triffle & their need of them will be great. I would thank you to present my respects to Mr. Telfair & let him know that his son's boxes & trunk have arrived safe. His son, Josiah, in my opinion, is equal if not superior to any youth of his years whom I have ever taught both as to genius and application, I do not hesitate to say that if he lives & is continued at study, he is capable of making a figure in the republic of letters. Master Thomas is also improving very desirably & I doubt not will be very clever. I shalt do myself the pleasure of addressing a line to Mr. Telfair in a short time. I am, dear sir, in much haste.

Your sincere friend,

Geo. Jones, Esq.   Moses Waddel[6]

In the Augusta Chronicle, September 28, 1799, Abraham Baldwin announced that the academy would open for its second year in Applington "under the care and instruction of the Revd. Moses Waddle." The Academy had become very well known and attracted very gifted students. A promising youth assisted him, one William H. Crawford. John C. Calhoun, another who revealed much potential, was under Waddel's tutelage. In 1797, the pupils held a culture exposition which was attended from as far away as Old Petersburg, Two plays were performed and 15 speeches made.

Waddel's Academy lasted until 1800, when he moved to South Carolina. His name will always be one of the first to be mentioned when education in Columbia County is discussed. It is no surprise that he later became president of the fledgling Franklin College in Athens, Georgia. As John Donald Wade wrote:

> Dr. Waddel was an extremely successful teacher. He had to a remarkable degree the knack of getting work out of all the youngsters under his charge. His boys revered him and loved him. [7]

If he might be called the father of education in the county, he and Abraham Baldwin, who drew plans for a state education system and a state university, might be termed fathers jointly of Georgia education! About Baldwin, the Augusta Chronicle, April 4, 1807, wrote, "He originated the plan of the University of Georgia, drew up the charter, and with infinite labor and patience, in vanquishing

66

all sorts of prejudices and removing all obstructions, he persuaded the Assembly to adopt it."

Another interesting person who taught school in the county in the 1790's was a mysterious Dr. Bush. He surfaced here at that time and for some reason wanted to cover his tracks, so to speak, for he had changed his name.   He was David Bushnell of Connecticut, a Yale graduate and veteran of the American Revolution.   He had invented and used the first operational submarine, called the American Turtle, against a British warship. Afterwards, he was commander of the Corps of Sappers and Miners in the Continental Army.   He left Connecticut abruptly after the war and showed up in Columbia County, where he founded Citizen's Academy in Leah, a classical and scientific school.

He taught there for a time, then practiced medicine in Warren County until his death in 1826:

> An example of Yankee ingenuity at its best, Bushnell received the epithet "Father of Submarine Warfare" because he constructed the first practical functioning underwater vessel coupled with his naval mines and rudimentary torpedoes, Bushnell's vessel showed him to be a true pioneer in the development of undersea warfare.[8]

In Columbia County after 1800, there were four types of schools in the towns and villages: Academy and grammar schools; primary and common schools. The former were apparently set up by the wealthier citizens, those who owned the great plantations and had had the benefit of education themselves. The academy in Appling, which was Waddel's under new ownership, was a "good brick building ... a quarter mile west of the town. It has," according to Sherwood, "a Library and Apparatus (laboratory equipment for sciences) and some funds."[9] The building was a two story structure with a principal and two teachers in charge. Grammar school apparently was a preparatory school for the academy which was secondary education like modern high schools. The children of the elite families attended these schools.

Appling also had the Columbia Female Academy. Both were destroyed 75 years later in a disastrous tornado as reported by the Daily Chronicle And Sentinel, March 25, 1875.

The primary and common schools apparently were the same as the academy and grammar schools but for the middle class families. George White observed, "Common schools are in most of the settlements (in Columbia County)."[10] The 1840 Census reported the following figures on all these institutions:

	Schools	Students
Academies and Grammar Schools	6	240
Primary and Common Schools	8	165

The total county population in 1840 was 11,356. 410 students out of that count reveal that few youth were given the chance for education. The slaves, of course, could not be schooled by law.

The census perhaps did not record a phenomenon which started in the farming areas and was funded by the poorer farmers whose children could not attend the aforementioned schools. That phenomenon was the "Old Field School." This name took hold because that was exactly where the schools were located, in a field somewhere which was accessible. The farmers in a given area would come together, select a location, and build a clapboard, one-room structure where a hired teacher could teach all grades. To imagine this set-up, the reader need only peruse Augustus Baldwin Longstreet's Georgia Scenes, or Washington Irving's "Legend of Sleepy Hollow," or Richard Malcolm Johnston's Dukesborough Tales to conceive the more humorous side of these schools.

Yet, in their humor, these writers also give a very good description of the Old Field School system. Often times, the teacher was one of questionable repute who could read and write only, yet he still knew more than the children. Discipline was harsh, but the parents expected this. Most of the white children in the county, who had any schooling at all, probably went to these schools.

In the 1850 Census, only common schools were listed; there were 6 in the county with 260 pupils. The 1860 Census did not tabulate schools at all. The Civil War, as it did with every facet of life in the county, had a detrimental effect on education. "School attendance was irregular, for parents frequently kept their children at home to help with necessary duties."[11] Many of the male teachers went to the army or moved about among schools seeking better pay in the hard times of the war.

The Freedmen's Bureau helped the children of the ex-slaves who had had no education at all during slavery. It set up in Georgia 66 schools, 66 teachers, and 3500 pupils. There was one such school in Appling for the black children in the county, for the 1870 Census reported 17 Negro males and 25 females in school. This school was set up by Charles Stearns at his plantation: The teacher, Miss R.W. Stearns, wrote of it:

> It was on the 8th of January, 1868, that I commenced teaching. ... Three long and rather rough benches were brought in and ranged around the bright glowing fire, in the large open fire-place. They were soon filled by about 25 or 30 children and women .... They did not know the name of the first book, or of any other book in the Bible; they could not count five; they did not many of them know the names of a single letter. In short, they knew nothing.

This was not surprising that they would be totally ignorant, since the American brand of slavery did not permit slave literacy of any kind: "Never had no schools at all, didn' 'low us to pick up a piece of paper and look at it," remembered Nancy Boudry, ex-slave of the Jarrell Plantation in the county.[12] The aid of Northern philanthropists and the Bureau helped the Negro immensely in the Reconstruction.

The white children, on the other hand, fared worse across the state. In the county there were only 434 white pupils in school. Total illiteracy in the county in 1870 was staggering: 6,323 out of a cumulative of 13,529 persons of all races. Much needed to be done for sure, but remedies were slow in coming. By the turn of the century, the Census listed 1,338 white students and 1,032 Negroes in county schools, This is a total of 2,370 out of a total of 10,653, all races, in 1900.

The Lunchroom of Allen Grove School for African Americans, c. 1930's. (Courtesy of Elma Jean Lazenby.)

By then, the academies had largely disappeared since the wealth of the antebellum days had dissipated during the war. Cox Institute for Girls was at Forrest, however, in the 1880's. In the rural areas, the old field school tradition continued with students still taught in the one room building, one teacher instructing all grades. "The children were so uncomfortable in the buildings in the winter that school was usually held in summer and because many had to work on the farms, their attendance was irregular."[13] It was not uncommon for male students to go only as far as the eighth grade before having to go to work fulltime either on the farm or some other job.

Education

M.L. Duggan, Rural School Agent for Georgia, stated in a 1917 report, "The State apportions $3.35 per child per year for the education of your children. This very small sum will not buy much education for your children. They deserve more."[14] He also advised against the summer term because "the distractions of picnics, protracted meetings, etc., with the usual irregularities of attendance, is of little benefit to the children."[15]

Columbia County had by 1917 levied a county-wide local school tax to supplement the state apportionment mentioned above. The State Legislature had passed the McMichael Bill in 1906 which stated that an election could be called "and that a tax of not more than one half of one per cent could be levied if two-thirds of the voters favored it."[16] Columbia County was among the 41 counties which passed this tax.

In addition, the white schools of the county were governed by the following standards which were the beginning of a statewide move toward requiring accreditation:

I   The Teacher

1. Good teaching.
2. Good order and Management.
3. First Grade certificate.
4. Full, neat, and accurate school register.
5. Daily program posted in room.
6. Teacher's manual.

II   Grounds

1. Good condition.
2. Playgrounds
3. School garden.
4. Two separate sanitary closets.

III   Building

1. Painted outside.
2. Plastered, or ceiled and painted.
3. No leaks.
4. Windows without broken panes.
5. Cloak room.
6. Good doors with locks and keys.
7. Clean and well-kept.

IV   Equipment

1. Patent Modern Desks.
2. At least 20 lineal feet of blackboard per room.
3. Building comfortably heated and ventilated.
4. Framed pictures on the wall.
5. Dictionary, maps and library.

6. Sanitary water supply.

V   Associated Activities

1. Manual arts, corn, canning, pig, poultry, or cooking club.

VI   Salary of Teacher

At least $40.00 per month.

VII   Term

At least seven months. [17]

Those counties whose schools met these standards were presented a diploma from the State Department of Education. Columbia County was one such recipient.

These standards above may seem quaint to many readers, but for those who went to school as late as the 1940's, they hold special memories. In some cases the "dear old golden rule days" were anything but that. As strange as they seem, the fact that these standards were ever written indicates how poor some schools had become.

Education for the Negroes in the county was another story altogether. After Reconstruction was over, the help of the Freedmen's Bureau dried up and Jim Crow laws called for separate schools, if any at all. The Negro citizens were serious about education, for the experience of slavery had taught them that in education was freedom truly to be found. Tyranny over the mind to them was the worst form of bondage. Negro Bishop W. H. Miles, first prelate of the Colored Methodist Episcopal Church, when it was formed in 1870, stated this need for education among Negroes succinctly and cogently: "We must become a reading people ... next to maintenance of sound doctrine ... the vital point is the education of our people." The freed slaves almost intuitively sensed this need for education. Charles Stearns, a planter in the county, observed them:

"... our Sunday School now numbers over one hundred pupils, mostly adults; seventy-five of them have already purchased the National Primer ... Most of them spend their two hours' nooning which I give them, in learning their lessons, ..." [18]

When others would not help locally, they turned to religious institutions. All over the state it was not uncommon to see a one-room schoolhouse sitting next to a Negro church, as in the case of the Walnut Grove School which sat adjacent to the Walnut Grove church. The congregation helped fund the school and provide its teachers.

In 1907, the Anna T. Jeanes Fund was established to help rural Negro public education. In 1909, the Caroline Phelps-Stokes Fund was set up to help with salaries of black teachers. In 1917, the Julius Rosenwald Fund made its first priority the building of schoolhouses for Negroes. These outside sources were necessary. As Dorothy Orr wrote:

> Allocation of funds (by the counties in Georgia) to Negro schools for buildings, equipment, maintenance, libraries, supplies, and, in fact, every phase of education was a very small percentage of the allocations for the same purpose to the white schools.[19]

1940's picture of Pollard's Academy for African Americans in Harlem, Georgia. (Courtesy of Lallie Dozier Benkoski.)

Most of the schools for Negroes in Columbia County up to 1950 were built with Rosenwald funds, the teachers paid by the Phelps-Stokes fund, and the teachers largely recruited by the Jeanes Fund. One need only to visit the Walnut Grove school now preserved in Appling to see an example of a Rosenwald building. Worn now with age and neglect, the one-room cabin at first was new and clean. The children sat on benches by grade until desks could be bought. One teacher taught all grades up to the seventh. There was one outdoor toilet for the girls.

Other such schools were Pollard's Academy, Galilee, Mt. Moriah, Winfield, China Hill, Steiner Grove, Spring Grove, Popular Springs, Bailey Grove, Lamkin Grove, Smith Grove, Mt. Enon, Mt. Olive, Macedonia, Water Branch, Gospel Water, Jerusalem, Oakey Grove, Solid Rock, Clary Grove, Allen Grove, Appling Elementary, and Sardis.

Of special interest in the saga of Negro education in the county is the Rosemont Baptist Association, a group of churches near Pollard's Corner. This group established its own school called Rosemont High School or Academy (1900 –1913). It also set up a fund for scholarships around 1900 to aid those students who wanted to further their education.[20] The sad fact is that after 1913 in the county there were no high schools for Negroes. If the student wanted higher education, he or she had to attend either Paine Institute or Haines Normal Institute in Augusta. The Walker Baptist Institute, which started in Waynesboro, eventually moved into Augusta and provided secondary education. These efforts at Negro education in the county paid a dividend in the 1930 Census: out of a total of 5536 Negroes in the county, only 881 were illiterate. Some of the stellar leaders in Negro education here were George C. White, Nancy Brinson, Mary Sanders, and William Lampkin. An elementary school in Harlem was named for Reverend White; after integration the name was changed to South Harlem Elementary.

There were schools for whites in Winfield, Harlem, Grovetown, Appling, Evans, and Leah. In the upcountry, Leah and

Winfield had schools with eleven grades, so the students who finished the school in Appling had to go to either of these to finish their secondary education. Some of the white teachers were Mary Weeks, Catherine Blanchard, R.O. Eadie, H.O. Henderson. These older white schools were slowly replaced by a building program initiated by county vote, June 9, 1954. Eight new school buildings were built, including those for the black students under the "separate but equal" rubric of the time. John Pierce Blanchard, county school superintendent, was the prime mover in this project.

Winfield High School was torn down in 1950's. It is pictured here as it looked around 1900. (Courtesy of Lallie Dozier Benkoski.)

In the 1950's, the climate of education began to change with the advent of a leader who loved children, saw their educational needs, and was aggressive enough to make certain the commissioners of the county also saw these necessities. If Moses Waddel, as this writer thinks, was the father of education in historic Columbia County, then the father of education in modern Columbia County was John Pierce Blanchard. An educator of long tenure himself, he knew the assets and debits in the county education system. From his work as principal of Leah School, he became county superintendent of schools. He was particularly interested in the debits in the cultivation of the Negro students.

It was his leadership which brought the first Negro high school into the county. Before then, as has been shown, the Negro students desiring higher education had to go to private black schools, taking with them their considerable talents and potentialities. Blanchard High School on Columbia Road was the result of his work.

Blanchard was quick to seek out talented black teachers. One of these was Mrs. Mary Sanders who had completed her education and was teaching out of the county in Thomson, Georgia. He called her, she remembers, and said that her home county needed her talents more than McDuffie County did and brought her back home to finish her tenure of fine instruction in Harlem. She later became a member of the county Board of Education.[20]

Four new schools were also made for the Negro students which did away with the one-room accommodations that had prevailed: Blanchard High (as already mentioned), George T. White Elementary in Harlem, Phinizy Elementary, and Gibbs Elementary near Evans.

John Pierce Blanchard was the newly elected superintendent of schools in 1949. (Courtesy of Pat Blanchard.)

76

Education

On May 17, 1954, Chief Justice Earl Warren and the United States Supreme Court struck down all segregation laws in the nation in the Brown vs. the Board of Education of Topeka. Integration was slow in coming, however, especially in the deep South. It was finally mandated in the 1970's, but Blanchard, ever the visionary, saw it coming and during the 1960's started integrating the county schools.

In April, 1966, he sent out letters to all parents of school-age children which included a list of the schools. His injunction was that the students should opt for the school they desired, "no matter whether that school was formerly a white or a Negro school," as reported in the COLUMBIA NEWS, April 28, 1966. It was a signal moment in the long history of education in the county. Superintendent Blanchard took a stand when it was most unpopular to do so, making a few enemies along the way, but great men do what has to be done, when it needs to be done, whether they like it or not.

Today, the public education system in the county is second to none anywhere, with new schools being constructed to accommodate the influx of people moving into the area. The schools are as listed:

Belair Elementary

Blue Ridge Elementary

Brookwood Elementary

Euchee Creek Elementary

Evans Elementary

Grovetown Elementary

Harlem Elementary

Martinez Elementary

Riverside Elementary

South Columbia Elementary

South Harlem Elementary

Stevens Creek Elementary

Westmont Elementary

Columbia Middle School

Evans Middle School

Harlem Middle School

Lakeside Middle School

Crossroads Academy

Evans High School

Greenbrier High School

Harlem High School

Lakeside High School

On July 8, 2000, the County Historical Society unveiled in Appling a memorial to John Pierce Blanchard which will remind future students of the legacy he created. As Preston Sparks wrote of the dedication, <u>News Times,</u> July 12, 2000, Blanchard "is credited with transforming the county's school system from a rural operation into one of the best in Georgia.

WALNUT GROVE SCHOOL

Chapter Three Footnotes

[1] E. Merton Coulter, "Ante Bellum Academy Movement in Georgia," Georgia Historical Quarterly 5 (1921), 12.

[2] Dorothy Orr, A History Of Education In Georgia (Chapel Hill: University of North Carolina Press, 1950), 21.

[3] Revolutionary Records.

[4] Coulter, 12; W.J. Northern, Men Of Mark In Georgia II (Atlanta: Caldwell, 1910), 392. Mt. Carmel, near Willington, South Carolina (where Waddel later had a very renowned academy) is not to be confused with the Carmel Academy near Appling; see Augusta Chronicle, July 17, 2000.

[5] Coulter, Ed. "Waddel's Memoir," Georgia Historical Quarterly 8 (1924), 304-305. Waddel does not mention his Georgia experience. See also L.L. Knight, Reminiscences Of Famous Georgians II (Atlanta: Franklin-Turner, 1908), 119 and Coulter, Old Petersburg And The Broad River Valley (Athens: University of Georgia Press, 1965), 153-154. "... many presbyterian ministers by conducting schools were enabled 'not only to secure a better support ... but also do something' as teachers," Wade Crawford Barclay, Early American Methodism 1769-1844 I (New York: Board of Missions and Church Extension of the Methodist Church, 1949),222.

[6] Moses Waddel to George Jones, Savannah, December 15, 1798. Ms. in Southern Historical Collection, Chapel Hill, North Carolina.

[7] John Donald Wade, Augustus Baldwin Longstreet: A Study Of The Development Of Culture In The South (New York: MacMillan, 1924, 24. See also Margaret Coit, "Moses Waddel,

A Light in the Wilderness," <u>Georgia Review 5</u> (Spring 1951), 34-47.

[8] Evelyn Cherpak, "David Bushnell," <u>American National Biography</u>, eds. John Garraty and Mark Carnes (New York: Oxford, 1999), 85-86. Keith Whitescarver, "Creating Citizens for the Republic: Education in Georgia," <u>Journal Of The Early Republic 13</u> (1993), 455-479. <u>Webster's American Military Biographies</u> (Springfield, Massachusetts: G. & C. Merriam Company, 1978), 52.

[9] Adiel Sherwood, <u>Gazateer Of Georgia</u>, 54.

[10] <u>Statistics Of The State Of Georgia</u>, 193.

[11] T. Conn Bryan, <u>Confederate Georgia</u>, 226.

[12] Mildred Thompson. <u>Reconstruction In Georgia</u>, 34; <u>The American Slave: A Composite Autobiography 12</u> (Westport, Connecticut: Greenwood, 1972), 114.

[13] Orr, 250.

[14] <u>Educational Survey Of Heard County</u> (Atlanta: Department of Education, 1917), 6.

[15] Duggan, 5.

[16] <u>Acts And Resolutions Of The General Assembly Of The State Of Georgia</u>, 1906, 69, 101.

[17] Duggan, 28.

[18] W.A. Bell, <u>Missions And Cooperation Of The Methodist Episcopal Church South With The Colored Methodist Episcopal Church</u> (Nashville: Commission on Cooperation and Counsel, 1933), 44-46. <u>The Blackman in the South, and the Rebels; or the Characteristics of the Former, and the Recent Outrages of the Latter</u> (1872; reprinted, New York, 1969), 162.

[19] Orr, 312.

Bibliogrpahy

[20] Leslie Pollard, <u>Complaint To The Lord: Historical Perspectives On The African American Elderly</u> (Selingsglove: Susquehanna University Press, 1996), 109, 245. The association initially helped the elderly as Pollard points out. See also Robert G. Gardner, "African-American Institutions in Georgia," <u>Viewpoints Georgia Baptist History</u> 16 (1998), 25. Another source in <u>Viewpoints Georgia Baptist History</u> 14 (1994) states that the Rosemont Baptist Association began in 1904 and lasted until 1910 (38). This conflicts with contemporary sources which show the Association very much alive, though perhaps unconnected with the statewide group.

[21] Personal Interview, May 14, 2000.

To Seek a Newer World

—Chapter Four—

Religion

OLD KIOKEE BAPTIST CHURCH
APPLING, GA. ···EST. 1772.

When the English first came to found the colony of Georgia, they brought their state religion with them-The Church of England or the Anglican Church. At that time, people took their religion more thoughtfully and seriously than today. Personal theology was a very strong thing to them, and a sense of exclusiveness was very real regarding those who professed a different idea of things eternal or spiritual. The Anglicans had come to espouse the position of theologian Jacobus Arminius, a Dutch churchman, who took on the predominant Calvinism of the day. Calvinistic thinking can be best understood with the acronym TULIP:

Total Depravity

Unconditional Election

Limited Atonement

Irresistible Grace

Perseverance of the Saints

What this meant was that man cannot reach God across the great gulf which separates them, which is the true meaning of the word "depravity." God, then, takes the initiative, reaches across that gulf, selects whom He wishes to save, which is unconditional; thus atonement is limited to those elected ones. His grace is irresistible to the elect; in other words, whether they want it or not, they are bowled over by His grace, and they must persevere in their elected state.

Arminius saw several things wrong with this system:

1. Those not "elected" go to hell despite what they do.

2. There is no assurance of divine election.

3. Man is a helpless pawn in God's hands.

4. If one is "elected," he cannot be otherwise, hence he can do as he pleases morally.

Arminius determined that not only was man not a pawn, he also had freedom of the will to exercise as he will, and grace was free. He in addition can have a hand in his own salvation, which is called "synergism." Now, all of this to a Calvinist was nonsense, bordering on heresy. What it all amounted to for the layman who had little time to delve into theology systematically was that one was either a Calvinist or a despicable Arminian!

From this theological cauldron sprang the major denominations of Episcopalians, Presbyterians, Baptists (some of whom were Arminians), and Methodists. The last two had the largest impact on Columbia County. Since the writer of this present history is Arminian (Methodist), he will deal with them first!

George G. Smith wrote:

> In 1757, the Society of the Church of England, for the propagation of the gospel, sent out missionaries to the colony in Georgia, and Jonathan Copp came to this distant mission (Augusta), which was on the frontier of the English settlements in America, A church was built at the expense of the colony on the lot on which St. Paul's Church now stands. [1]

At that time, there were no Methodist churches in the Parish. Methodism, with its preaching of free will and assurance of personal salvation, was suited to the rugged pioneer who enjoyed the air of freedom in his lungs and mind. But Methodism was late in coming to the upcountry. In 1786, fourteen years after Kiokee Baptist Church was built, two Methodist missionaries appeared in the Kiokee area. It was not exactly friendly territory, for neither the Baptists nor the Anglicans cared much for these "enthusiasts," as they were termed.

"The Methodists," wrote a Presbyterian-turned-Methodist minister,"I know, are a people that are set at naught by many, but for my part I hope to live and die in fellowship with them." Indeed one could be thrown out of a Separate Baptist congregation for becoming "a General Baptist (Arminian), Methodist, deist, or universalist." [2]

Thomas Humphries and John Major, the two Methodist preachers, attracted many by their preaching, including the attention of William Few, Sr. He "joined the Methodist Church the first year that its preachers crossed the Savannah River Viz in 1786." [3] The patriarch Few, Sr. was very influential in starting a

Methodist society in the upcountry, even building what was known as "Few's Meetinghouse" in the old Brownsborough area. [4]

This tabernacle, or brush arbor, was the central meeting place for the Methodist at the White Oak Campmeeting site. Built in 1873, it is still actively used by the United Methodist denomination. (Courtesy of the Josie Dozier Collection).

This church would be, then, the first Methodist one in upper Columbia County. As Brownsborough slowly dissipated, so did Few's congregation, as nothing remains there today. The congregation may have become a part of White Oak Methodist Church, which was ongoing in 1792 in the village of that name.

One of the signal experiences of the year for the Methodists was that of gathering for two or three weeks at campmeeting. A brush arbor served early on for the preaching, with families dwelling in tents around it. This phenomenon was a product of a wave of revivalism which was sweeping the southeast. One such site was White Oak Camp Ground. Bishop James Osgood

Andrew, whose parents had lived in the county, while living in Augusta for a time, remembered fondly a visit he made to White Oak Campground in the 1820's:

> The congregation was very large, variously estimated at five to ten thousand persons ... It was an awfully glorious time. Scores rushed to the altar for prayers; many went stricken to their tents, and there sought the aid and counsels of Christian friends; and not a few sought retirement in the solitude of the forest...[5]

The term "campmeeting" came from Kentucky as early as 1799; as one participant wrote afterwards:

> The meeting on the Muddy River ... was attended by a large concourse of people from far and near, They came on foot, on horseback, and in wagons, and camped on the ground. This meeting was the origin of campmeetings in the United States.[6]

White Oak Campground is still in service today, its tabernacle and cabins replacing the old brush arbor and tents of former times. An interesting story about the campmeeting there and the famous Charleston earthquake of the 1880's has it that as usual at campmeeting, village boys would wait in the woods around the tabernacle to watch the girls, as boys are wont to do. When the earthquake struck Charleston, the shocks were felt even in the Augusta area. When the ground quivered around the tabernacle, the boys were frightened out of their wits and as one they all rushed to the altar in fright, if not repentance.

Elisha Perryman wrote in his autobiography of one of the first real "characters" in early Methodism:

> Lorenzo Dow, a sort of wild man, came through the country preaching. His first appointment in our neighborhood was at Columbia courthouse (Appling). A great many people went out to hear him ... Dow was a great curiosity in almost every way, [7]

The Methodist Church grew in numbers during the antebellum period, with missions to the slaves and growth in every area of its life and mission. In 1844, on a national scale, however, the agitation over slavery was such that the denomination split over Bishop James Osgood Andrew of Georgia owning slaves. The Bishop had inherited slaves through his marriage and abolitionist-minded Methodists thought it repugnant. The ill-fated 1844 General Conference, after heated and pernicious debate, resulted in the Southern delegates walking out and forming the Methodist Episcopal Church, South.

The new denomination redoubled its efforts to evangelize the slaves, and in Columbia County, the Columbia Mission was organized expressly for the bondsmen.[8] By 1860, there were 9 Methodist churches in the county, on a circuit served by two pastors, with a total wealth of $22,000. The white membership was 420; the slave membership was 375. Obviously, some of the wealthy plantation owners were Methodists! In 1865, however, there were 441 white members and 260 freedmen; the wealth of Columbia County in 1865 was not given in the annual reports, but it was considerably less. The Methodist freedmen, although some stayed in the MECS, wanted their own denomination, however, and in 1870, petitions were made to the General Conference to form such. Out of this grew the Colored (now Christian) Methodist Episcopal Church, There are two in the county now, Jones Chapel and Woodlawn.

In Appling, there was a Baptist Freedmen's Church which met in the old Masonic Hall, in addition to a CME church. In the1875 tornado, both of these were destroyed, along with Kiokee Baptist Church. The Negro Methodist minister, Isham Jackson, afterwards held services for both Baptist and CME Negroes in the courthouse which itself had lost its gables and roof, as reported in the <u>Augusta Constitutionalist</u>, March 21, 1875. Judge William Gibson in Augusta printed a plea in the March 25, 1875 <u>Chronicle And Sentinel</u> for the people of that city to help raise money to aid those affected by the tornado.

It must be said regrettably here that the history of Southern Protestantism is not a happy one in the matter of race relations, which is remembered now as a dark, diabolical period in denominational histories of all the white branches. At the turn of the century, 1900, Klanism was latent and insidious in the major Protestant denominations, Methodist and Baptist. There are disturbing accounts of "ministers leading their congregations in hunting down victims, of colored men being lynched in church yards, of ladies selling grisly pictures of lynched, mutilated bodies in order to raise church funds ..."[9] According to a story in the Augusta Chronicle, June 25, 2000, Klanism is still around, not latent but distressingly visible.

The major white Methodist denominations reunited in 1939; in the 1960's the Evangelical Brethren were included and today we have the United Methodist Church. The United Methodist Churches listed below begin with the historic congregations and proceed to the latest. Few's Meetinghouse has already been discussed as possibly the earliest in Columbia County.

White Oak United Methodist Church was founded in 1792 by Bishop Francis Asbury who traveled all over the eastern states by horseback or chaise, a marvelous man, indeed. He visited White Oak church again in 1796 and 1800 and 1803. The present building is a renovation of the 1803 structure. Also, on the 1803 visit, Asbury spent several days in the home of Ignatius Few.

It may be that the nucleus of the White Oak congregation actually was the society which met at Few's Meetinghouse in1786. According to Rev. Hubert Story, one of the families of the first congregation at White Oak was the Thomas Ansley family; he was a first cousin to the founder of Methodism, John Wesley, He is buried in the church cemetery. The nearby White Oak Camp ground has endured the years and is still a favorite campmeeting site for area Methodists.[10]

Shiloh United Methodist Churchwas founded c. 1838 in Winfield, Georgia. (Courtesy of Lallie Dozier Benkoski.)

Shiloh United Methodist in Winfield is another very historic congregation. The Georgia Historical Commission marker in its front yard proclaims:

> Shiloh Methodist Church, the outgrowth of the earliest known Methodist place of worship in this community, has had a church building on this site for over 125 years. Originally services started by a local hermit "who lived by a spring," were held in a "brush arbor" about a mile west of here. A short time later a church was built on this site, a short time later after this church was completed, two plots of land were deeded to the four commissioners of the Methodist meetinghouse. One, including the hermit's spring, was from Waters Briscoe, the other, including the site of Shiloh Church, was from Green Dozier. The present church building was erected in 1857.

This "hermit" reminds one of the "wild man" Lorenzo Dow, a powerful Methodist preacher, but a bit eccentric in appearance and behavior. He did not fit the "proper" mold of a Methodist divine and was not the most popular man at Annual Conferences, if indeed he deigned to attend. Variously called "crazy Dow," "crazy preacher," "wild man," and "that eccentric preacher," it is not inconceivable that he was indeed the hermit who started Shiloh Methodist Church, He walked everywhere he went and lived on the good charity of the people. An account of Dow's visit to Appling courthouse has already been mentioned in this chapter. George Gilman Smith, in his Hundred Years Of Methodism In Augusta, described Dow thus: " He was dressed in a strange garb and behaved in a strange way. He carried no baggage; he carried a lot of tracts, which he distributed as he went. His hair and beard were long and unkempt ..." [11] But there was power in his preaching. He could get things done, like paying off the debt on St. John's Methodist Church in Augusta.

Dunn's Chapel in Leah, Georgia, is one of the early Methodist congregations founded in the 1840's by John Dunn, a local preacher, and a local native. He preached in Citizens Academy until a structure was built. The Academy was also called Dunn's.

Harlem Methodist Church has had an interesting odyssey.

> The history of the Methodist Church in Harlem and the history of the town are inseparable. The original center of the community in this area was called Saw Dust. The church there was Mt. Tabor which still stands and is now a Baptist Church. The congregation at Mt, Tabor during the early years as a Methodist Episcopal church numbered about 30 or 40 persons and the pastor was The Rev. George D. Hardaway. He was succeeded by The Rev. Wm. W. Oslin, who was the grandfather of Ernest, Hulon and Evelyn Hatcher. The church at Harlem was organized about 1874 and the first structure was built that year and dedicated by Bishop Pierce in 1875. The deed to the land where the church now stands is recorded in the office of the clerk of the Superior Court of Columbia County dated June 17, 1879. Since the Harlem community was founded as an escape from the vices and problems of the saloons and night spots of Saw Dust, the churches were established as a part of the original development of the town.

91

The second church building was built in 1902. It was a beautiful structure with a large bell tower and a bell which was used to call persons to worship from all over the community. This building burned in 1928 from over heating in the heaters. This tragedy was a severe blow to the church and the community and is spoken of even today with great emotion by those who experienced it. Services were held temporarily in the Star Theater until a new structure could be erected. The new church building was begun immediately and was ready for use in 1929. That building is the present sanctuary having been renovated in 1968.

The Methodist Church in Harlem was described in an early issue of the <u>Columbia Sentinel</u> as having " ...always been in the front ranks in fighting for right, endeavoring to emancipate the ignorant, taking care of the youth, while beating back the power of sin and darkness at home and ... in foreign fields."

Mary Wilcox
Secretary

Harlem United Methodist Church now has an imposing structure and an active congregation.

Philadelphia United Methodist Church was organized in 1840. G.B. MaGruder deeded the land for the building. Like Harlem Methodist, this congregation was built around a nucleus of an earlier church.

Marvin United Methodist Church was chartered in 1891. At first, a small country congregation, it now is in the middle of the growth of population in the Martinez area and is growing rapidly.

Lewis Memorial United Methodist Church "began around 1900," according to church historian Lou Ann Penland. "Mr. William Ellis Lewis donated the land ..." It was first named Sardis Methodist but in 1947, the local church conference changed it to the name it bears today, Lewis Memorial. Sitting at a crossroads of Columbia Road and Hereford Farm Road, the church like Marvin above has been a recipient of the urbanization of the county. A bigger sanctuary and education plant was built in the 1990's. It celebrated its centennial in 2000.

Grovetown United Methodist was founded in 1880. According to Kathy Ruddy in her excellent book on the Grovetown Methodist Church,

> ... it was time to establish a permanent meeting place for Methodists in the Grovetown village. A three-sided structure was built on a clearing owned by Dr. Joseph Hatton. It had a tented top and an open side which faced the main road (now known as Robinson Avenue). It was used for semi-regular worship from 1880 until the spring of 1881 when the tented top was replaced with a roof, a fourth wall added, and better arrangements could be made for more regular attendance by a minister or passing preacher.

Other historical Methodist churches and missions, some of which no longer exist, were Adams Chapel, Friendship, Mann's Memorial, The Rocks (later Pierce's Chapel), Reid's Chapel, Belair, St. Mary's, Linwood, Pace's Chapel (Martinez), and Evans Mission.

Jones Chapel and Woodlawn Christian Methodist Episcopal (1881) Churches at Winfield and Harlem respectively are outgrowths of the founding of the CME denomination in 1870. When the tornado of 1875 destroyed the CME church in Appling, Jones Chapel was built in the vicinity.

The growth of population in Columbia County, already alluded to, has fostered the need for more Methodist churches in the Martinez-Evans area of the county. Starting in the 1950's the following "recent" churches are in full swing for the Lord: Martinez United Methodist (1959), Riverview UMC, and Wesley UMC (1990), which has 1300 members.

Jones Chapel C.M.E. Church near the White Oak community. The Christian Methodist Episcopal denomination was begun in 1870. (Courtesy of Lallie Dozier Benkoski.)

One of the first groups to arrive in the wilderness of the upcountry which later became Columbia County settled around Kiokee Creek near what was later Appling. Into this settlement came a Separate Baptist minister named Daniel Marshall. His theology had been deeply influenced by the preaching of Methodist evangelist George Whitefield; "awakened by the preaching of Whitefield, (he) believed in evangelism, and joined in that work.... They were called 'Separates' by virtue of their practice of repudiating the principle of church establishment and seeking a more spiritual and Biblical worship..."[12]

Going against the establishment, in this case, the Church of England which was the "state" religion of the Georgia colony, was risky business. Marshall was actually brought to court to explain his impudence. It is an interesting thing to see that in Marshall's case, the Baptists learned much from the upstart Methodists! He organized in 1772 the first Baptist church in Georgia, Kiokee Baptist, and constructed a rude log meetinghouse, as they called church buildings then. In October 1784, the Georgia Baptist Association was founded there which became the Georgia Baptist Convention. In December, 1789, Kiokee Baptist Church was incorporated and called, interestingly enough, "The Anabaptist Church on Kiokee." In Appling later on, a brick structure was built. Harris and Mosteller's monumental church history of Kiokee, one of the most comprehensive this present writer has ever come across, details the development of this famous church.

It must be added here that Daniel Marshall and his son, Abraham, were always concerned about the spiritual welfare of the Negro. In Savannah in 1788, for example, Abraham did an unheard of thing by ordaining a Negro named Andrew Bryan. Note the date, 1788. This was long before the Methodists or any other denomination reached out to the slaves. For years at Kiokee Baptist, the two races worshipped together, albeit separated, but under the same roof. The reader may call this crass paternalism and what-not, but the motivation on the part of the Marshalls was the care of the Negro's immortal soul. For that, if nothing else, Daniel and Abraham and others who shared their sentiments, stand tall in the annals of evangelical Christianity.

Sharon Baptist Church in Winfield, Georgia was founded by Abraham Marshall in 1799. (Courtesy Lallie Dozier Benksoski.)

Sharon Baptist Church—Abraham Marshall founded this church in 1799 at Winfield. Like the other churches of all denominations up to and through the Civil War, whites and Negroes worshipped together. This, of course, ended with the fall-out of the war. Sharon remains an active church, having survived the storm.

First Mt. Carmel Baptist Church, Winfield—According to the church historian,

> In the year of our Lord 1873, October 13th, about seventy members under council from Sharon Baptist Church received permission to organize the first Mt. Carmel Baptist church. Before the first house of worship was built, the members had access to the house of worship owned by Sharon Baptist Church for more than two years. Reverend E. D. White was elected as first pastor and served until his death, a period of 29 years. ,., The mortgage burning

ceremony for the new building was held on January 1986,
...

New Holt Missionary Baptist Church was organized July 13, 1868 at Harlem. Reverend Aaron Green was the first pastor, according to Mary E. Sanders, church clerk. Melvin Adams is the present pastor. The church has been a leader in community improvements in the past decade.

First Mt. Moriah Baptist Church, Appling—It is postulated that this church was originally started by Negro members of Kiokee Baptist, that they met in a building in Appling which was destroyed by the 1875 tornado.[13] The present structure was made around 1890, but historically, it is one of the oldest Negro churches in the county. Kiokee Baptist Church influenced the genesis of several other churches in the county:

Red's Creek or Abilene—According to the church history published in 1999:

> In 1774, he (Loveless Savage) founded the Reed's Creek (Abilene) Baptist Church near a tributary of Reed's (also spelled Red's) Creek. It was at this location, just northeast of the intersection of Old Petersburg Road and Old Evans Road, where the first site of the church, along with a cemetery was located. [14]

Harris and Mosteller suggest that the nucleus of this congregation might have been the congregation of Quaker Springs, which had been "gathered by Daniel Marshall." [15] The church was moved to where it is now on Washington Road in Martinez where it enjoys a new sanctuary and educational plant and a growing membership.

Grove Baptist Church—Founded in 1808 on Synagogue Road under the aegis of Kiokee Baptist, this congregation was moved in 1853 to the southern part of the county where the Georgia Railroad ran through the area. The church and its community became the nucleus around which the city of Grovetown was to grow.

Bethel Baptist Church—Founded in 1830 in the community of that name, the church prospered for a time and during Reconstruction and afterwards was the headquarters of the local chapter of The Grange, a farmer's organization as discussed in Chapter 2 of this history. "By 1873, the church had 34 white members and 88 Negroes for a total membership of 122." [16] In 1937, the church was declared defunct, however, and the property bought by Kiokee Baptist.

Damascus Baptist Church—Founded in Leah July 29, 1820, by Samuel Cartledge, this church was pastored by Juriah Harriss from 1846-1850. Harriss was considered one of the remarkable pulpiteers of his time. He was very prominent in his neighborhood and "at ordinations, marriages, and burials, his services were always in demand." [17] Reverend Harriss, however, was but carrying on the legacy of Cartledge, who was converted by the preaching of Daniel Marshall. The founder of Damascus Church was also a great pulpiteer: "His knowledge of the Bible was remarkable. His sermons were interwoven with passages of scripture, accurately quoted, and illustrative of the views presented." [18]

Rosemont Baptist Association—Second Mt. Carmel Baptist Church and several other Negro churchs formed this group which has been discussed in Chapter 3 of this history.

Old Evans Baptist Church in Evans, Georgia picture here. (Courtesy of Dan Marshall.)

Evans Baptist Church— "the official birth of the church took place on August 10, 1930 at a meeting in Evans Public School. Ten members of the Abilene Baptist Church had tried for several months to gain financial assistance and sponsorship from the Abilene Church for the establishment of a church in Evans. Unsuccessful at this attempt, the ten members of the church met at the public school building with Rev. J.C. Myditt, a retired minister, Rev. Gill and Rev. W.H. Danner, all of Augusta. The families made plans to build a building for worship and education across from the public school at Washington and Belair. The land had been donated by the Clark and Clark Real Estate Company of Augusta. The church proceeded to gather the material for construction of stucco building." [19]

Harlem Baptist Church—This church was founded in 1874. The building was the point from which the city limits extended three-tenths of a mile around.[20] An interesting lesson here, for the church <u>should</u> be the center of town!

Mt. Tabor Baptist Church—See Harlem Methodist Church earlier in this chapter for information on this congregation.

Other Baptist churches are as follows:

Old Union – 1845	Grace – 1972
Water Branch – 1874	Mount Olive - ?
Cobb Grove – 1872	Mount Enon - ?
New Hope – 1887	Solid Rock - ?
Second Mount Moriah – 1887	Steiner Grove - ?
	Walnut Grove - ?
Cedar Grove – 1890	Gospel Water Branch - ?
Powell – 1893	Oakey Grove - ?
Bethesda – early 1900's	Simonia - ?
Fountain Grove - 1954	

Moses Waddel was appointed to Mt. Carmel Presbyterian Church in Columbia County, April, 1794. He has already been discussed in Chapter 3. The First Presbyterian Church in Augusta was chartered in 1804. Waddel's church then would be the first in the area. A Presbyterian sanctuary in the Appling area after Waddel's time has not been mentioned or at least not found in any records. Kiokee Baptist records do say that in 1863, the Presbyterians used their old building and wanted to buy it later, but the Kiokee Trustees would not sell it to them. What happened to these Presbyterians is not known. Today, the BelAir Presbyterian Church and the Korean Presbyterian Church, both in Evans, and the Grovetown Presbyterian carry on the tradition set by Waddel.

Today, there are upwards of one hundred churches in the county of all denominations and faiths. The growing international look is seen in the Islamic Society of Augusta in Martinez;

Swaminarayan Temple (Hindu) in Evans; Baha'l Faith of the CSRA in Martinez; and the Korean Presbyterian Church mentioned above. As the urbanization of the county continues, more churches undoubtably will be necessary. The fact that the county has a sister city in Poland also underscores the internationalism. It is well that this communication across racial, cultural, and religious boundaries occurs, for the county cannot and will not survive in an isolationist environment, The historical churches discussed earlier in the chapter merely set the stage for a wider outreach.

In conclusion, there is a church mentioned in an old slave narrative of 1936 in which Cora Shepherd, a former slave of the Jesse Walton plantation, says:

> "Us went to white folks' church—sat in the back," she said.
> "And it was the beautifullest place! The water down the hill
> jus' spewin' out! It was called Greenbrier Church, near
> Cedar Rock." [22]

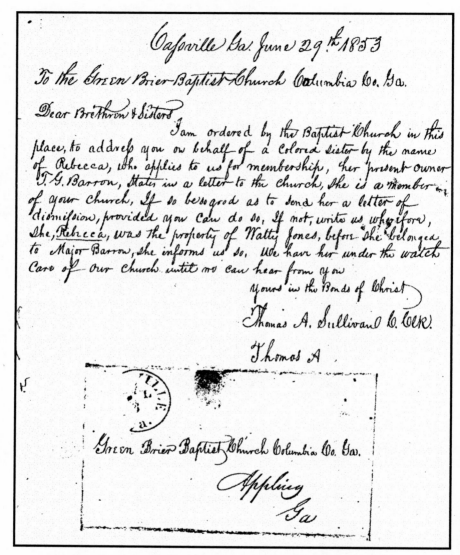

Cassville Ga. June 29th 1853

To the Green Brier Baptist Church Columbia Co. Ga.

Dear Brethren & Sisters

I am ordered by the Baptist Church in this place, to address you on behalf of a Colored sister by the name of Rebecca, who applies to us for membership, her present owner T. G. Barron, states in a letter to the church, she is a member of your church, If so be so good as to send her a letter of dismission, provided you can do so, If not, write us why:fore, She, Rebecca, was the property of Watt: Jones, before she belonged to Major Barron, she informs us so, We have her under the watch Care of our church untill we can hear from you

Yours in the Bonds of Christ

Thomas A. Sullivan C. Clk.

Thomas A.

Green Brier Baptist Church Columbia Co. Ga.

Appling

Ga

A careful search of available sources yielded no clue to the identity of this church nor location. Harris and Mosteller's work on Kiokee Baptist history did not mention such a church. It was even thought that this old slave, 82 years of age, might have been mistaken. However, quite by accident, the following letter from

Cassville, Georgia, in 1853 was addressed "To The Greenbrier Baptist Church, Columbia Co. Ga." in Dan Marshall's collection. Further investigation revealed that her memory of a waterfall of sorts was quite correct, for on Greenbrier Creek near Appling the water indeed does tumble over a bed of rock. It may well be, also, that Cedar Rock was a community in the county. The letter also reveals that slaves actually carried their church letters whenever they were sold to other areas:

> Cassville Ga. June 29th 1853
> To the Greenbrier Baptist Church Columbia Co. Ga.
> Dear Brethren & Sisters,
> I am ordered by the Baptist Church in this place, to address
> you on behalf of a colored sister by the name of Rebecca,
> who applies to us for membership, her present owner T.G.
> Barren, states in a letter to the church, she is a member of
> your church, If so be so good as to send her a letter of
> dismission, provided you can do so, If not, write us
> wherefore, she REBECCA,was the property of Watty
> Jones, before she belonged to Major Barren, she informed
> us so, We have her under watch care of our church until we
> can hear from you
> Yours in the bonds of Christ
> Thomas A. Sullivan, C.Clk

George Walker Crawford also established a church, of unknown denomination, on his Bel Air estate. It apparently was absorbed by another congregation for it no longer exists. Shortly after the death of Paul Hamilton Hayne in 1886, near Grovetown, the Episcopal Church of Heavenly Rest was built and dedicated in his honor and memory. The church no longer exists. Trinity Episcopal Church in Harlem was founded in 1954.

ADDENDA

Since the foregoing text was written, more information has come to light regarding the early Methodists in the County. Few's Meeting House has been mentioned in connection with the early Methodist missionaries and William Few Sr.'s conversion to Methodism. His meetinghouse was located within the confines of old Brownsborough and may have later become Mt. Carmel Church.

Another Methodist society and meetinghouse was formed at the home of Thomas Haynes on Uchee Creek near present day Windmill Plantation around 1788. It was subsequently called Kiokee Society, though not related to Kiokee Baptist church. It, as with Few's Meetinghouse, was visited several times by both Bishop Francis Asbury and Lorenzo Dow.

The mystery of the Presbyterian presence in the early days of the county was clarified by Reverend Harold Lawrence:

"Presbyterian efforts in Columbia were strong in the period of the 1790's. The Richmond Creek congregation was formed in 1788; Carmel and Joppa by 1796; and the Great Kiokee congregation was also from an early period," (Early Societies in Upper Georgia (Tignal, GA: Boyd Publishing Company, 1997), 137.

OLD KIOKEE
BAPTISMAL POOL

Chapter Four Footnotes

[1] George G. Smith, <u>A Hundred Years Of Methodism In Augusta</u> (Augusta: Richards and Shavers, 1898), 5.

[2] Quoted in G.G. Smith, <u>Life And Letters Of James Osgood Andrew</u> (New York: Trow, 1882), 19-20, <u>Strength For Today, Bright Hope For Tomorrow: Abilene Baptist Church, Martinez, 1774-1999 Georgia</u> (Franklin, Tennessee: Providence House, 1999), 26

[3] Florence Fruth, <u>Some Descendants Of Richard Few Of Chester County, Pennsylvania</u> (New York: McClain, 1977), 21.

[4] Plat Book A, p. 190, Columbia County Courthouse.

[5] <u>Life And Letters Of James Osgood Andrew</u>, 129-130. See also William H. Sparks' description of a campmeeting in Greene County, Edward Cashin, ed., <u>A Wilderness Still The Cradle Of Nature: Frontier Georgia</u> (Savannah: Beehive, 1994), 23.

[6] A.H. Redford, <u>History Of Methodism In Kentucky I</u>, 266.

[7] <u>A Wilderness Still In The Cradle Of Nature</u>, 50.

[8] <u>Minutes Of The Annual Conferences Of The Methodist Episcopal Church South II</u>, 61.

[9] Robert Moats Miller, "Southern White Protestantism and the Negro, 1865-1965," Wynes, ed. <u>The Negro In The South Since 1865: Selected Essays In American Negro History</u>, 238.

[10] Letter from Hubert Story, Pastor, White Oak UMC, June 1, 2000.

[11] E. Merton Coulter, <u>Old Petersburg And The Broad River Valley Of Georgia</u> (Athens: University of Georgia Press, 1965), 161-163, <u>One Hundred Years Of Methodism In Augusta,</u> 12.

[12] Harris and Mosteller, 22.

[13] Mosteller and Harris, 164-165.

[14] <u>Strength For Today Bright Hope For Tomorrow</u>, 42

[15] Harris and Mosteller, 198.

[16] Harris and Mosteller, 201.

[17] Harris and Mosteller, 147.

[18] Tony W. Cartledge, "Samuel Cartledge: Colonial 'Saul of Tarsus,'" <u>Viewpoints Georgia Baptist History 8 </u>(1982), 24.

[19] John Miller, Evans Baptist Church, 1930 – 1980, 14.

[20] <u>Acts And Resolutions Of General Assembly Of The State Of Georgia, 1870.</u>

[21] Harris and Mosteller, 90.

[22] Ronald C. Killion, ed., "Reminiscences of the 'Peculiar Institution,'" <u>Sandlapper 5</u> (October 1972), 50.

—Chapter Five—

*T*owns and *V*illages

CEDARVALE
LAND GRANT FROM KING GEORGE III
WINFIELD, GEORGIA

The earliest village in old Columbia County was Brandon, founded by Edmund Gray in 1751. This community did not last long, although it appears on a map of 1779. In the 1770's, several more villages sprang up, the largest of which was Wrightsborough which for a time was a prosperous town. Both of these sites are in present-day McDuffie County, along with the site of Friendsborough. One can still visit the Rock House and a few

109

reconstructed cabins near Thomson which are the only remnants of old Wrightsborough.

In the confines of present-day Columbia County, one finds the sites of Brownsborough, Kioka, and Cobbham (which is on the county line with McDuffie). For these, see Chapter 2. Of particular interest, however, is the reference by Moses Waddel to the community of Carmel which does not appear on any known map (see Chapter 3). One is almost compelled to find Carmel where Old Washington Road crosses, by bridge, Greenbrier Creek (see Jubal O.Marshall to Cornelius Collins, Deed Book Z, p. 449), Columbia County Courthouse.)

Other settlements in the county are virtually in name only. The 1853 map of Georgia which General William T. Sherman used to draw the lines of march for his forces to the sea shows in Columbia County, excluding those villages now in McDuffie County, Eubanks (which according to the map's key had a post office), Appling, White Oak, Berzilia, and Belair, all of which also had post offices, albeit some post offices were in houses. Fortunately, Sherman did not consider these of any consequence!

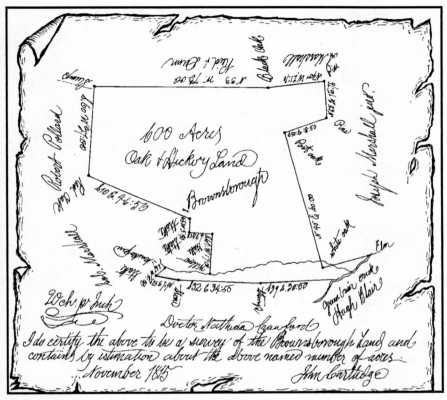

According to an 1895 map, there were Ramsey, Eubanks, Delph, Hazen, Cluese, Berzilia, Kioka, Parnell, and Forrest. Quaker Springs, also called Quaker Settlement, is not on a map and is known only today because of a small part of a cemetery which was to be moved because of progress.[1] Lewiston, which does appear on modern maps, is a crossroads community on Columbia Road where is also located Lewis Memorial UMC. Campania now has New Hope Baptist Church to mark the community site. A place called Sewallville is mentioned on an 1870 affidavit.

Pumpkin Center, at a crossroads near Harlem, is listed on modern maps. At one time, it was a little community with four stores, a blacksmith shop, four dairies, and cotton gins, according to AUGUSTA CHRONICLE, September 21, 1987. There was also a baseball field there in the 1890's. White Oak community at one time had a post office and stores, in addition to the Methodist Church and adjacent campmeeting ground. Phinizy, which is on current maps, and Winfield are small communities in the historic upcountry; Hazen and Cluese were also in that area.

Berzilia and Forrest Station were on the Georgia Railroad between Harlem and Grovetown. The former was on an 1852 map with Appling, the only two towns shown; it had a hotel for train passengers, a lawyer's office and in the 1890's was the site of the Georgia Railroad's employee's picnic and recreation facilities. Both had a few stores and houses. Forrest had for a time Cox's Institute for girls. Near Harlem and Grovetown also were the communities of Bel-Air, Cerlaste, Westview, Bugg's Crossing, and Ellis. Up near Little River, Mistletoe Corners, now in the state park of that name, was a "once thriving community," according to the COLUMBIA NEWS AND MARTINEZ-EVANS TIMES, July 28, 1971. Evidence was found in the park of old chimneys, foundations, and steps, and even, Heavens above, several moonshine stills. The same is true for a little community and post office site near Appling named Delph: some foundations in the underbrush mark its once busy homelife. A letter with a "Delph" postmark is in the Dan Marshall collection.

The monument of Daniel Marshall is situated in the center of this view of Appling's Main Street. (Courtesy of the Josie Dozier Collection.)

As was seen in Chapter 2, the land for "Applington" was deeded in 1792. After the hurrah over where the county seat would be located, Cobbham, Kioka, orAppling, the latter eventually won the honor. The court house and jail were built in 1812, before the village was chartered four years later. In 1827, Adiel Sherwood wrote that Appling had grown to include "fifteen houses and stores, Court House, Jail and Academy." In 1829, he came back through and observed three stores, the same fifteen houses, courthouse and jail and Baptist and Methodist churches.[2] He fails to mention the post office. By 1875, when a tornado swept throught the area, Appling had grown to include a Negro Methodist church and a Negro Baptist church,in addition to the two mentioned above. The Columbia Female Academy and the Columbia Academy (for the young men) were both there, although the former had ceased as a school and was a tenant house. There were by then numerous houses and stores. A stagecoach tavern and inn which sat directly behind the courthouse on the stage road. The house survived the tornado but gradually fell to pieces and was razed in 1998. Its old chimney still stands.

The tornado, which destroyed many houses, the two academies, and stores, apparently was a watershed mark in the history of the county seat, for the town never quite recovered. The fact that it was miles from the nearest railroad also was detrimental to its hope for prosperity. Today it is still the county seat for a while longer, and when court is in session, the village is busy once again. The offices of county government are there, as are the Board of Education and Public Health Department offices. The new detention facility is nearby. A new post office was built in 1967, and a bank was opened in the 1980's.

The future of Appling is not good since the seat of county government and a new courthouse are destined to be in new facilities in Evans. Members of the county historical society and others interested in the county's great past are determined to keep Appling as a historic site, where tourists may find a sense of nostalgia and a taste of history.

An interesting facet of Georgia history is the development of towns and cities that would not have been at all were it not for the railroads. The state history is replete with such instances. On the other hand, one can also see the demise of many communities. In Columbia County, Appling and other upcountry villages are good examples of "dying on the vine," so to speak. When the Georgia Railroad was laid out through the southwest portion of the county, 1834-36, there were no substantial towns or villages. The railroad needed water and wood for the engines; therefore, at various places along the tracks, several miles apart, there were lumber piles with accompanying sawmills, plus watertanks. These needed people to operate them, and the people put up shacks to live in.

Such was the inauspicious beginning of Harlem, Georgia. Around 1836 and 1840, after the tracks were laid, lumber crews were stationed at that particular spot to prepare fuel for the trains. So much was required that sawdust piles heaped up; hence the name "Sawdust" was given to the settlement of workers and their families. A Methodist church was built there which later became the nucleus of the Harlem Methodist Church, chartered in 1874. The town father was a former engineer, Newnan Hicks, a devout Methodist. His residence-hotel, built a mile from Sawdust and its rather loose reputation, became the catalyst for the new town.

This is a remarkable c.1900 postcard of the City of Harlem. Notice the wagon wheel ruts in the dirt road. (Courtesy of Darwin Morris.)

On October 24, 1870, the General Assembly of Georgia chartered the new town; it was named for the borough in New York City—Harlem.[3] Its location had not escaped the attention of the people in the area. On February 19, 1865, the <u>Augusta Chronicle And Sentinel</u> stated that geographically it was

> ...said to be one of the prettiest locations for a town in the country around - celebrated for its remarkable healthy position, fine water, and beautiful groves. A number of citizens, determined not to be cramped up in the dust and heat of city life, have laid out a town, and will soon commence to put up for themselves, comfortable cottages, dwellings, and proclaim their independence of high rents and city extortions.

A firm belief in prohibition also caught the eye of many who wanted to escape the more damaging aspects of living in a big city. The churches in Harlem were staunch in opposition to the devil's brew and the word got around that this made the town, among other assets, a rather good place to raise children. The <u>Columbia Sentinel</u> could boast on April 19, 1881:

> As a health resort, Harlem is without a peer. We have unequalled railroad facilities, telegraph and express office, the purest water, but twenty- five miles from Augusta, a beautiful soil, a lovely country, Methodist and Baptist churches, a fine school, and the cream of society.

Business flourished at the turn of the century. Two banks, first in the county, a drug store, a grocery, <u>The Columbia Sentinel</u>, founded by Reverend J.M, Atkinson, and his other newspaper <u>The Farmer's Light </u>were products of Harlem. An opera house was there for the culturally minded. A phone exchange was developed. The Columbia County Cotton Oil Company was started; electric lighting was introduced. The town was advertised as a progressive, resort place, ideal for people who wanted a nice place to live.[4]

Harlem was the home of Oliver Hardy, Sr., the Tax Collector of the county for many years. "It is hard to resist," wrote H.R. Casey in the COLUMBIA SENTINEL, April 25, 1883, "that good open jolly, funful face, round as the full moon, and covered all over with smiles, ... this Falstaffian figure ... is as polite and

116

graceful as a French dancing master..." If this description reminds one of Oliver Hardy, Jr., born in 1892, then well it might. "The branch does not fall far from the tree," the old saw goes. Oliver, Jr. may be Harlem's most famous son, one-half (the largest half) of the Laurel and Hardy movie team with a square in the famous walk of stars at Grumman's Chinese Theater in Hollywood. The Hardy Festival in October of each year in Harlem brings hundreds of visitors to commemorate this great person.

Laurel and Hardy impersonators ride in a Model T Ford in the Oliver Hardy Festival in Harlem, Georgia. (Courtesy of the City of Harlem.)

In 1901, O.B. Stevens wrote, "The most thriving towns in the county are Harlem and Grovetown."[5] Yet, Harlem was not without its sad moments. The Depression affected its banks and finances; a terrible train accident in the city, April 14, 1910, claimed several lives; a massive conflagration virtually erased the downtown area, November 31, 1911, causing many thousands of dollars in damage. But the little town had the muscle and fortitude to overcome all these and still remains a bright spot in the county.

The Tracy-Luckey Pecan Factory is well-known in the Southeast for its gift packages of pecan delicacies.

This picture shows the U.S. Post Office and neighboring store in Martinez, Georgia, in the 1930's. (Courtesy of Carole Davis.)

Martinez-Evans—In 1892, the Charleston and Western Railroad laid tracks through the eastern part of the county and gave rise to two such stops as mentioned with the genesis of Harlem. The first station was named Jenkins. Another stop a few miles further on was named Evans (see Chapter 2). Over the years, these became small communities with post offices, a few stores and houses. Evans also had a Baptist church and a Methodist mission.

Jenkins was near the old colonial Quaker Springs settlement which had, because of its spring and its location on Washington Road, an inn-tavern for the passengers on the regular stages which came through. The railroad took care of the stageline in short

One of the wealthy landowners at the turn of the century was a Cuban named Martinez Y'Saldivar, a very popular and successful Hispanic. For a time, Jenkins became Lulaville, named for one of Saldivar's daughters. It was later named for Saldivar himself and called as it is now Martinez, although the pronunciation has been Anglicized.[6]

For many years, it remained an insignificant little village, not to be compared favorably with Harlem, Grovetown or even Appling. In the 1950's however, as shown in Chapter 2, things began to change radically with the advent of Clark Hill Lake, Fort Gordon (1940's), and Savannah River Site. Thousands began to purchase acreage for homes in that part of the county until today, the suburban sprawl has eradicated all vestiges of the original Martinez and has spliced its name with Evans.

Picture here is Polatty's Cities Service Gas Station in Evans, Georgia, c. 1940. (Courtesy Griffith Polatty.)

Evans was a small village with some stores and houses. For once in its insignificance then, it was the center of the county's attention when in 1909, President William Taft and a party of officials stopped off to meet county dignitaries and enjoy some good barbecue. He certainly was no stranger to good food and was well pleased with his afternoon visit. Dr. John Miller wrote:

> In the 1930's the Evans community was still rural in nature. Roads were unpaved. There were few automobiles. Horse-and-wagon was the primary means of local travel. Travel, for any distance, was conducted by train. A railway depot was located in Evans. W.E. Polatty, Sr., whose family would later become a part of the Evans church, was station manager.[7]

The erstwhile little village has been transformed with the housing industry and residential neighborhoods. Its post office, once in a cabin, has now doubled its output in a new building as has Martinez. The sprawling county government complex, banks, real estate firms, lawyer offices, facilities for the elderly, theaters, myriad gas stations, and shopping centers have, as with Martinez, done away with the small village setting. One wonders why neither Martinez nor Evans, since this phenomenal growth, have been incorporated, mayors elected, and city councils set up.

The high density of the population has also transformed the law enforcement resources. Where there once was a sheriff and two deputies for the entire county, there now is a force of hundreds of lawmen, with attendant transportation facilities. The density has also taxed the resources of the waste disposal landfill.

Grovetown—The Grove Baptist Church was founded in 1808 by Abraham Marshall under the aegis of Kiokee Baptist and moved to the southern part of the county in 1853 near Wrightsboro Road, which, by then, was a main artery for delivering tobacco from the upcountry to Augusta.[8] A small community had sprung up around the Georgia Railroad to service the engines of the trains; a water tank, lumberyard with sawmill, and a depot had been constructed. The Grove Church became a part of this community

120

which, according to one writer, was called simply "Sunnyside." When Paul Hamilton Hayne moved there in 1865 and had his "Copse Hill" home built, he addressed his correspondence as simply "Georgia Railroad," signifying the depot where the train picked up and dropped off the mail.[9] His presence there as the South's most significant man-of-letters brought considerable activity when famous writers like William Gilmore Simms visited his humble cottage.[10]

By the 1870's, word had gotten out to the Augustans along the Savannah River that the little town, called "Groveton" by then, offered relief from the miasmas of the summer. As Mrs. Rosa Owens stated in the News-Times, May 17, 2000, "Many people aren't aware that Augusta owes Grovetown because at one time diseases were killing people there from yellow fever, malaria, and typhoid fever. They rode their wagons and buggies here to get away from the air downtown."

In 1881, the town was incorporated, still under the name of Groveton:

> That, from and after the passage of this Act, the town of Groveton, in the county of Columbia, shall be a body corporate, with the corporate limits of said town extending one and a half miles in every direction from the Georgia railroad depot in said town. ... That Dr. Joseph Hatton, John N. Fisk, Charles Clifford, Charner H. McDonald, Ulysses R. Brooks, be and they are hereby appointed Commissioners of the town ...[11]

In the late 1880's, the town took on the aspect of a resort area. The railroad and accompanying depot were a ready access for visitors to the town and the Grovetown hotel was built to provide not only lodging but luxury. Christened first as the "Rosalind," the name subsequently changed to "The Eagle," Jesse Thompson built the stately edifice and left nothing to the imagination: He had a cupola where visitors could view the countryside; an indoor rink for roller skating, a sport sweeping the nation at the time; and a magnificent rotunda which was used variously for recreation, church gatherings, and dances.

A Methodist church came in due time to supplement the work of the Grove Baptist Church. The pastors had much to look after, for Grovetown was fast becoming a resort town with attendant evils. For the entertainment of tourists who came in "by the cars," J.L. Dodge built a dirt race track adjacent to his magnificent Dodge House for sulky racing. His thoroughbred horses, the envy of any in Kentucky, were a source of wonder.[12]

The photographer who took this c. 1900 photograph of the J.L. DodgeHouse in Grovetown, Georgia, was standing in a sulky racing track adjacent to the house. (Courtesy of G.J. Smith.)

When Camp Gordon was established in 1941, Grovetown began to enter the modern age. Its population steadily increased as it became a bedroom area for service families who wished to live "off the post." Its depot and facilities saw much traffic during the years of World War II and the Korean War. Many children perhaps stood spellbound as flat cars of tanks and other materiel of war lumbered through on the rails. Georgia Iron Works, Grovetown's most stable industry, saw much work during these times.

The Grovetown Museum, under the work of Rosa Owens and Charles Lord, was opened officially on May 27, 2000. It contains mementoes of the beginnings of the town, the war years, the schools, and strives to accumulate other items which will ensure that the history of the city will be preserved for future generations.

Leah – Located above Pollard's Corner on the edge of Thurmond Lake, this community does not appear on the 1895 map mentioned above but was an old town nevertheless. It has some stores (bait and tackle primarily), Dunn's Chapel UMC, Damascus Baptist Church and Rehoboth Baptist Church. At one time, it had Citizen's Academy and a high school.

Pollard's Corner – This crossroads appears on modern maps and serves as a retail and gas outlet for patrons of Thurmond Lake. The Pollard's Lumber Company, of course, is there.

REESE MARSHALL "FIXIN" TO CARRY MAIL IN HIS "TIN LIZZIE". (CIRCA 1920)

To Seek a Newer World

Chapter Five Footnotes

[1] Several members of a lady's family were disinterred to make room for a turn lane on Washington Road, May   2000. Residents of the area who grew up around the site of old Quaker Springs report that at one time the cemetery was very large. Unfortunately, many graves may be now under asphalt.

[2] Sherwood, Gazateer Of Georgia, 54.

[3] Acts And Resolutions Of The General Assembly Of The State Of Georgia, 1870.

[4] Columbia Sentinel, July 23, 1908.

[5] Georgia: Historical And Industrial, 613.

[6] Augusta Chronicle, October 4,1987.

[7] John Miller, "Evans Baptist Church 1930 – 1980," N.D.N.P., 3.

[8] Harris and Mosteller, 200.

[9] Edwin Mims, "Paul Hamilton Hayne," Library Of Southern Literature 5 (Atlanta: Martin and Hoyt, 1907), 2269.

[10] Others who visited Hayne at Copse Hill were Sidney Lanier, Henry Timrod, Maurice Thompson, and editors of famous literary magazines.

[11] Acts And Resolutions 1881, 487.

[12] Margaret Rodgers, Historical Landmarks And Legends Of Columbia County (The County Historical Society, 1976), n.p.n.

To Seek a Newer World

126

—Chapter Six—

$\mathcal{B}$usiness and $\mathcal{I}$ndustry

STAGE COACH INN

Although Columbia County has had some forms of industry all along, Pollard's Lumber Company and the Quarry, for example, the hard truth is that for a time, the industry of Augusta and Richmond County had obviated the need for the same in Columbia County which was fast becoming urban. More workers commuted out of the county than worked within it. In 1977, less than 50% worked inside the county's confines. In agriculture and forestry, in the decade of the 60's, the county was behind the nation; in the industries of mining, construction, manufacturing, and services, the county led the nation.

In 1976, the following were the leading industries in the county:

TRW, Martinez

Georgia Iron Works, Grovetown

The Thomson Company, Martinez

Tracy-Luckey Company, Harlem

The Thomson Company, Harlem

Johns-Manville Club Car, Martinez

Georgia Vitrified Brick and Clay Company, Harlem

Augusta Iron and Steel Works, Martinez

Sudan Industries, Martinez

Verdery and Sons, Inc., Harlem

Kaykor Company, Martinez

Of these, the Thomson Company and the Vitrified Brick are no longer in service. The latter, founded in 1902, produced clay items such as fire brick and what became known as "Augusta Block," a paving brick or cobble which was used in cities as far away as Tampa, Florida. Sewer pipe was also made. The loss of the company is keenly felt. The Tracy-Luckey Company, founded in 1937, is a leading pecan industry in the state with branches in Albany, Georgia, and Hickman, Kentucky. Its gift packages are a staple Christmas gift item all over the Southeast.

In 1999, there were over 149 firms in agriculture, forestry, and fishing. The close proximity of Lake Thurmond with its opportunities for boating, fishing and wildlife observation, in addition to seasonal hunting opportunities for deer and turkey has added much to the business climate. The camping facilities of the reservoir have also brought in businesses which cater to the needs of campers; boating dealerships have been built in Martinez-Evans. Automobile businesses are specializing in Recreation Vehicles. Off-road biking has become a viable business opportunity.

The dam on Clark's Hill Reservoir, now called Lake Thurmond, is on the Savannah River. (Courtesy of W.C. Blackard.)

In the recreational field, also, is that of the golfing sport, with two new golf courses in the Martinez-Evans area. Stores to outfit the golfers have multiplied. As more and more retirees move into the area, these courses, with those of Richmond County, will be very popular, and more courses will be in the offing. The downside of this will be the usage of the land. In the field of recreation also, Patriots Park is now known over the Southeast as premier sports arena, attracting people from all over. This promises to continue as more and more sports tournaments are hosted. This, of course, brings income to the area and potential residents.

Though it may seem strange to consider land usage in the chapter on business, it is relevant. As the Good Book stipulates,

"In all thy getting, get understanding." Shelter belts of forestry must be preserved to prevent erosion and flooding. The prehistory along Kiokee and Euchee Creeks should be preserved as much as possible. The inherent natural beauty of the county should be preserved and enhanced. Development of the land for business is a necessary corollary for progress, and no one would rationally attempt to stop it, but careful and insightful planning is necessary as shopping centers and urbanization only promise to get larger in proportion to the growing population.

The housing industry has been and continues to be a stable asset in the economy of the county. Pollard's Lumber Company and Georgia Pacific are two of the largest suppliers of this field. Suburbs are planned generally to take the best advantage of the natural beauty of the location. The increasingly high density of the county's population will demand more and more of these suburbs. Growth will continue, as indeed it has already started, to reach into the "upcountry" of the county, around Appling. So, the housing industry will remain strong.

The area of public education in the county employs hundreds of faculty, administrators and staff, thus being one of the county's largest businesses. New schools, undoubtably, will be needed with more faculty and so forth. Again, wisdom is necessary in mapping the expansion of these schools to take best advantage of terrain as well as suburbs.

Law enforcement is a huge business as more and more lawmen will be needed to keep pace with the urban growth and attendant problems. The materiel needed by a large police force is awesome, but the county must again keep pace with its growth. State-of-the-art equipment and transportation obviously are a sine qua non for an effective security force.

Retail outlets such as Home Depot, Lowe's, K-Mart, Walmart and hundreds of others are important in the county's growth for the revenue they generate and the out-of-county patrons which they attract. The commodities outlets such as Krogers, Food-Lion, and

130

Bi-Lo with many such others also generate important revenue, and all of these offer employment opportunities. The restaurant and fast-food industry also attracts hundreds of consumers and employs hundreds of persons. The many departments under the broad umbrella of county management offer employment in many areas.

At this point, a word regarding the state of politics in the County is necessary for it impacts heavily on the growth of the County. For years, the Democratic Party has been dominant in our history. An interesting thing has happened: The erstwhile ideals of the Democrats, conservatism, states rights, etc., are now espoused by the Republicans (see Chapter 2). In the last twenty years, the latter have come to power in the County. Interesting to the historian, for essentially, the party of Lincoln has become the party of Jeff Davis! My, my! Whatever, party politics, schisms, and the "good ole boy" syndrome must not impede the growth of a fine county with a promising future. To be fair and just to all, there should be more African Americans on the boards of commissioners and education. As more Asians and Hispanics move in, they also should be thus represented.

All of the foregoing suggests to a county historian that Columbia County is certainly one of the fastest growing counties in the Southeast. With this, however, come growth pains which will be felt very severely if the county does not maintain its sensible, viable growth plan. Problems of waste disposal, drinking water, sewerage, infrastructure—all of these are the stress points which must be maintained at a high predictive level so that potential problems may not only be accounted for in long range planning but also obviated by clever foresight. The hope and dream of seeking a newer world lie on the shoulders of everyone in the county, from the chairman of the board of commissioners to the high school student who "shovels" hamburgers at McDonald's.

A newer world beckons us; the work of the founding fathers laid the foundation; the horrors of five major wars, Reconstruction, Great Depression and a myriad other problems have rendered us a wiser, tougher people. The influx of new potential and talent has

131

made us a more gifted people. A new spirit of cooperation among races and nationalities has made us a more inclusive people. The major religions represented in the county have made us a kinder and more respectful people. A newer world beckons; as Winston Churchill so rightly observed, "Let us go forward then in our united strength."

TAKING THE TOBACCO TO MARKET IN A "HOGSHEAD"

The Rest of the Story

Following are short biographical sketches of the historic personages mentioned in the early history of the county, with no attempt to include everyone, which would take volumes.

DANIEL APPLING—Born August 29, 1787, in Columbia County, to John and Rebecca Carter Appling, he was thoroughly educated at Citizen's Academy in Leah by Dr. David Bush (Bushnell), He joined the United States Army in 1805 as a lieutenant and was active in the Indian wars. In the War of 1812, he was raised to lieutenant -colonel for his bravery and leadership in the battles of Sandy Creek and Plattsburg in 1814 at Lake Erie. He died suddenly, March 18, 1818. In memory of him, the name of the county seat in Columbia County was changed from

Applington to Appling and on December 15, 1818, a new county was created and named Appling in his honor.

JESSE MERCER—Born December 16, 1769, in North Carolina, he came with his father Silas to the county where they became involved with Kiokee Baptist Church. Jesse became a minister and became most likely the most well-known Baptist preacher and educator of his day. He edited and owned The Christian Index, which was instrumental in founding the Georgia Baptist Convention, founded Mercer University (first at Penfield, Georgia, later at Macon), and published the first Baptist hymn book. He died September 6, 1841. Three excellent articles on Jesse Mercer are in Viewpoints Georgia Baptist History: C. Ray Brewster, "Jesse Mercer's Cluster," 8 (1982), 33-50. J.R. Huddleston, "Jesse Mercer's Influence on the Georgia Baptist Convention," 3 (1972), 41-66. Gregory Wills, "Jesse Mercer and Church Discipline," 14 (1994), 17-22.

WILLIAM HARRIS CRAWFORD—Considered by many scholars to be the greatest man Georgia has ever produced, Crawford was born February 24, 1772, in Virginia, but spent his childhood and early adulthood in Columbia County. He attended Moses Waddel's academy near Appling, after which he was a rector of Richmond Academy for a short while. He read law and was admitted to the Georgia Bar. Moving to Oglethorpe County, he practiced law until 1807 when he was elected to the U.S. Senate to finish out the term of Abraham Baldwin who had died in office. From then on, Crawford was in the national limelight: Senator, Secretary of War, Minister to France (where he won the accolade of Napoleon Bonaparte), Secretary of the Treasury, co-author of the Monroe Doctrine, and candidate for the Presidency (a stroke during the campaign forced him to step out). Returning to Georgia, he was appointed Judge of the Northern Circuit of the Superior Court, He died of heart trouble, September 15, 1834. He was a man of the times, not hesitating one moment to fight a duel if necessary. Crawford, Georgia, in Oglethorpe County, near his home and where he is buried, was named for him; so was Crawford County.

IGNATIUS ALPHONSO FEW —Born in the county, April 11, 1789, he studied law at Princeton and served as a colonel in the U.S. Army in the War of 1812. He entered the Methodist ministry and rose to great prominence in Georgia Methodism being the founder and first president of Emory College, later to be Emory University. He was the leader of education in the Methodist Church in Georgia. He also is responsible for the little town of Oxford, Georgia, where Emory College was instituted. He died of lung disease, November 28, 1845, and is buried in Oxford, Georgia. Ignatius Few needs an authoritative biography. For a good discussion of his connection to Emory College, see Henry Morton Bullock, <u>A History Of Emory University</u> (1936).

SILAS MERCER—Born in North Carolina, February 1745, he migrated with his family to this county where his distinguished son Jesse was raised. An eminent Baptist minister, connected with the history of Kiokee Baptist Church, Silas served as a chaplain in the American Revolution and was very influential in the Georgia Baptist Association. He died in 1821 from a kick in the head by a horse and is buried at Phillip's Mill Church in Wilkes County, Georgia. See J.R. Huddleston, "Silas Mercer: Founder and Father," <u>Viewpoints Georgia Baptist History 51</u> (1976), 65-79, for an excellent study of this man.

DANIEL AND ABRAHAM MARSHALL—For excellent biographies of these men, see Harris and Mosteller's splendid study of the founding of the preeminent Baptist church in Georgia, Georgia's First Continuing Baptist Church. Also, see James N. Griffith, "Remembering the Marshall Family," Viewpoints Georgia Baptist History 10 (1986), 9-18. The contribution of the Daniel Marshall family to Georgia Baptist formation and continuation cannot be minimized or overstated. Anything said by this author would only be a codicil to what has been written already.

WILLIAM FEW, JR.—Born in Maryland, June 81 1748, of William, Sr. and Mary Wheeler Few, he came with his family, after a sad time in North Carolina, to this county. His brother James had been hanged by the British after the battle of Alamance, North Carolina, May 16, 1771. This event was not calculated to instill love for the Tories, so William, his father, his brother Benjamin, and brothers-in-law were ardent patriots when the Revolution began in earnest. William, Jr.'s work in the county during and after the Revolution has been recounted in Chapter 2. In 1786, he was appointed by the state legislature to the national Congress; the next year he was in the famous constitutional convention which drafted that marvelous document the U.S. Constitution. His signature is on this document. He later served as U.S. Senator, state representative and Judge of the Second Judicial District in Georgia. He was an outspoken opponent of the infamous Yazoo Land Fraud. He moved to New York City in 1799 and was a member of that state body for four years. He was an officer in the Manhattan Bank and President of City Bank. He died on June 16, 1828, certainly one of the premier founders if not the father of Columbia County. An authoritative biography needs to be written on Few. For his own recollections, see C.C. Jones, Jr. "William Few, Lieutenant-Colonel Georgia Militia in the Revolutionary Service, with Autobiography of Col. William Few of Georgia, "Magazine Of American History (November 1881),

339-358. For the most recent biographical sketch, see Robert E. Wright, "William Few Jr.," American National Biography 7, 869-870.

MOSES WADDEL—Though not long in the county, his influence was indelibly stamped on the pupils he taught in his academy from 1796-1804 near Appling. He, as has been noted, combined teaching and preaching in his professional life and was always a very devout man. He taught in South Carolina at Willington after leaving the county. In 1819, he was asked to be president of Franklin College in Athens, Georgia (University of Georgia); he accepted and served as such until 1829. Returning to Willington, he taught there until a stroke partially paralyzed him. He died in 1840, July 21, in Athens. He was 70 years old. No more remarkable man in education ever lived.

GEORGE WALKER CRAWFORD—Born December 22, 1798, to Peter and Mary Crawford in Columbia County, he was second cousin to W.H. Crawford. Educated at Princeton, he returned to Augusta and read law under Richard Henry Wilde. He served in the state assembly for several years from Richmond County. Before that, he was Attorney General of the state. In 1843, he was elected to the U.S. Congress but the same year he was also elected by the Georgia Whigs as governor; he chose the latter and served two terms. Afterwards, he was Secretary of War under Zachary Taylor. As indicated in Chapter 2, he was honored to be the Permanent President of the Georgia Secession Convention in 1861. Retiring from public life, he built a huge estate named Bel Air just inside the Columbia County line on the Georgia Railroad. He also built a church for the community. He died in 1872 and is buried in the Summerville Cemetery. The house was razed when the Dyess Parkway was built in the 1990's. The church, too, has apparently not survived. For an unpublished biography, see "George Walker Crawford 1798-1872," Ph.D. dissertation, University of Georgia, 1972.

ROMULUS MOORE—Born into slavery of mixed parentage in 1817, he became a blacksmith. Learning to read and write, he purchased his freedom shortly before the Civil War and became a boardinghouse keeper and Baptist minister in Appling. The Freedmen's Bureau hired him to register black voters in 1866. After being elected to the Georgia House of Representatives in 1868, he with the other Negro solons were ousted, but later reinstated. He also served in the Constitutional Convention of 1867. After the violence of Reconstruction, he moved with other Negro families to Louisiana.

ABRAHAM BALDWIN— One of the most able men of his day, Baldwin was born in Connecticut, November 6, 1754. He graduated from Yale in 1772 and taught there until 1779. He studied theology for a while and served as a chaplain in the American Revolution, He came to Georgia, Savannah first, then made his home in Applington (Appling). He served for many years as representative then senator in the national Congress He was very influential in the 1787 national convention which framed the Constitution, which he signed with William Few, also of Columbia County.

A great man by any standard, he will be remembered in Georgia for his dream of a statewide educational program which would create a state university and have it control all schools supported by state funds. His dream was realized when Franklin College (University of Georgia) opened for business in 1801. He had drawn up the Charter, and his mind and heart are stamped indelibly on it. As he stated, the state must "place the youth under the forming hand of society, that by instruction they may be moulded to the love of virtue and good order." No republic is secure without a well-informed, educated constituency. Baldwin died in office as a senator from Georgia, March 4, 1807. For a complete biography of Baldwin, see E. Merton Coulter, <u>Abraham Baldwin: Patriot, Educator, And Founding Father</u>. Athens: University of Georgia Press, 1987.

EMILY TUBMAN—Born Emily Harvie Thomas in 1794, in Virginia, she lived for a time in Kentucky under Henry Clay's guardianship. She married in Augusta Richard C. Tubman in 1818 and at his death in 1836, she took over his large plantation near Appling and through keen business sense amassed a fortune. She gave much money to humanitarian interests, and her name is perpetuated in Columbia County by the road which bears her name. She died June 9, 1885, and is interred in Frankfort, Kentucky. A good sketch of her life is Martha Jacqelyn Craven's "A Portrait of Emily Tubman," <u>Richmond County History</u>, 6 (Winter 1974), 5-10.

PAUL HAMILTON HAYNE—Born January 1, 1830, to Paul Hamilton Hayne and Emily McElhenny Hayne, he attended the school of Christopher Cotes and College of Charleston. He began publishing verse in 1845, first in the Charleston <u>Courier</u>, later in <u>Southern Literary Messenger And Southern Literary Gazette</u>. He served as editor of <u>Southern Literary Gazette, Russell's Magazine, Southern Opinion, Southern Society And Augusta Constitutionalist</u>. His books of poetry were <u>Poems (1854)</u>, <u>Sonnets And Other Poems (1857)</u>, <u>Legends And Lyrics (1872)</u>, <u>Poems Of Henry Timrod (1873)</u>, <u>Mountain Of Lovers (1875)</u>, <u>Poems (1882)</u>, <u>Avolia, Lives Of Robert Young Hayne And Hugh Swinton Legare, And Live Of William Gilmore Simms</u> (unpublished). He died July 6, 1886 in Augusta. Rayburn S. Moore's <u>Paul Hamilton Hayne</u>, New York: Twayne, is Hayne's only biography and a good one.

OLIVER HARDY—Born in Harlem, Georgia, January 18, 1892, he became, as the world knows, the "bigger" half of the ever popular and famous Laurel and Hardy duo. Stanley Laurel, a British comedian, was teamed with him by Hollywood producers and the legend began. Hardy also starred alone in several movies, one at least with John Wayne, <u>The Kentuckian</u>. He died August 7, 1957, surely the most publicized Columbia Countian who ever lived, with the possible exception of William Harris Crawford. Each year, the Hardy Festival brings hundreds of people and Laurel-Hardy look-alikes. For at least one day of the year, everyone just has some fun.

JOHN PIERCE BLANCHARD—Born October 23, 1919, in Columbia County, Mr. Blanchard came from a long line of Blanchards in the county's history. He taught school in the county for years, serving as principal of Leah school until he became superintendent of schools. Under his leadership, the county built new buildings to replace the older structures, consolidated some, and integrated them all. He served as superintendent for 30 years during which time, public education here became one of the finest in the state. The John Pierce Blanchard Monument, sponsored by the County Historical Society, was unveiled with ceremonies on July 8, 2000, in Appling. Over two hundred persons attended, and many spoke of his perspicacity in leadership and his determination that all county youth would receive the best in education. He died August 27, 1992.

BILLINGTON McCARTER SANDERS—Born in the county, December, 1789, he attended what some historians refer to as Kiokee Seminary. Careful investigation has not turned up what this school was or where. The best possibility is that he actually attended Waddel's Academy which may also have been termed as Kiokee Seminary. He attended the state colleges in Georgia and South Carolina. He returned to Appling where he was rector of the Columbia Academy from 1811-1812; this was Waddel's school which had been relocated to Appling and named Columbia. After farming for two decades, he entered the Baptist Ministry through Kiokee Baptist Church. Interested in education, he became the first president of Mercer University. He was the moderator of the Georgia Baptist Association, and president of the Baptist State Convention. He died in Penfield, Georgia, March 12, 1852.

THOMAS EDWARD WATSON—Born near Thomson, Georgia, in 1856, he attended Mercer University and studied law. His stormy career included teaching, practicing law, championing the rights of farmers and all things rural, and serving in the Georgia House and the U.S. Congress. He wrote assiduously on many subjects, always a radical Democrat. In 1904, he ran for President at the head of the Peoples' Party. He died in 1925, one of Georgia's famous sons. A still definitive biography of him is C. Vann Woodward's <u>Tom Watson. Agrarian Rebel</u> (New York, 1938).

Appendix

Tributaries in Columbia County

Cliatt

Mims Branch

Keg Creek

Lake Springs

Lloyd's

Kiokee Creek

Little Kiokee Creek

Uchee Creek

Bettis Branch

Jones

Reed's

Rae's Creek

Butler's

Sandy Run

Boggy Gut Creek

Crawford

Greenbrier

White Oak

Burn's

Hayne's Creek

Cane (Germany)

Bohler

MAP OF INDIAN SITES

ENDANGERED SPECIES
OF COLUMBIA COUNTY

Animals

Common Name	
1. Peregrine Falcon (taken off in 2000)	Falco Peregrinus
2. Southern Bald Eagle	Haliaeetus lencocephalus
3. Wood Stork	Mycteria americana
4. Red Cockled Woodpecker	Piocoides borealis
5. Bachman Sparrow	Aimophila aestivalis

Plants

Common Name	
1. Little Amphianthus or Pool Sprite	Amphiamthus pusillus
2. Sun-Loving Draba or Open-Ground Whiltlow Grass	Draba aprica
3. Georgia Plume	Elliottia racemosa
4. Shoals Spiderlily or Cahaba Lily	Hymenocallis corondria
5. Mat-forming Quillwort	Isoetes tegetiformans
6. False Poison Sumac	Rhus michauxii
7. Sweet Pitcherplant or Red Pitcherplant	Sarracenia ruba
8. Ocmulgee Skullcap	Scutellaria ocmulgee
9. Granite Stonecrop or Dwarf Stonecrop	Sedum Pusillum
10. Relict Trillum	Trillium rehquum
11. Barbara's Buttons	Marshallia ramosa

FAUNA OF COLUMBIA COUNTY

<u>Mammals:</u>

whitetailed deer

black bear

bobcat

gray fox

red fox

raccoon

opossum

mink

longtailed weasal

cottontail rabbit

swamp rabbit

flying squirrel

fox squirrel

gray squirrel

meadow jumping mouse

ground hog

eastern chipmunk.

white-footed mouse

cotton mouse

golden mouse

eastern wood rat

least shrew

cotton rat

rice rat

muskrat

eastern mole

striped skunk

armadillo

hoary bat

brown bat

red bat

evening bat

coyote

Birds:

wild turkey	red breasted woodpeckers
redeyed vireo	pileated woodpeckers
towhee	downy woodpeckers
carolina wren	hairy woodpeckers
brown thrasher	mallard duck (migratory)
cardinal	canada geese
blue jay	peregrine falcon
mockingbird	southern bald eagle
wood thrush:	wood stork
tufted titmouse	owl
chickadee	
crow	
redtailed hawk	

Amphibian:

salamander	frog
toad	

Reptiles:

threetoed box turtle

loggerhead

skinks

Carolina pygmy
rattlesnake

northern copperhead

eastern cottonmouth

timber rattlesnake

midwest worm

eastern worm

northern black racer
snake

black king snake

scarlet snake

northern pine snake

midland brown snake

southern ringneck snake

gray rat snake

redbellied snake

eastern hognose snake

rough green snake

mole snake

corn snake

eastern diamond back

puff adder

indigo snake

Fish:

longnose gar	perch
Florida gar	Savannah darter
bowfin	shellfish
hickory shad	American shad
pickerel	hybrid
carp	eels
minnow	large mouth bass
shiner	redbelly
northern hogsucker	bluegill
catfish	red ear sunfish

FLORA IN COLUMBIA COUNTY

loblolly pine	vines
yellow pine	shrubs
white oak	canopy trees
blackjack oak	elms
beech	ash
tuliptree	basswood
red maple	hickory
silver maple	birch
walnut	black locust
black cherry	sycamore
sugar maple	cottonwood
herbs	pecan

mulberry

hornberry

American hornbeam

sweet gum

black gum

buckeye

Chinaberry

MINERALS OF COLUMBIA COUNTY

quartz

quartzite

basalt.

thyolite

argillite

tuff

kaolin

chert

soapstone

mineral talc

granite

feldspar

gold

Militia Organizations and Districts

Columbia County Officers are: Daniel Marshall, Tax-collector; Anderson Crawford, Receiver of Tax Returns; John Walton, Surveyor; John Pearre, Coroner. (From issue of Dec. 25, 1790).

Columbia County Militia Rank and Arrangement provided for by Executive order of January 20, 1791 (from issue of Jan. 24, 1791):

William Few, Colornel; Jesse Sanders, Lieut. Col.; William F. Booker, Major. Troop of Horse: Clam King Harrison, Captain; Yancey Sanders, 1st Lieut.; John Williams, 2nd Lieut.

    1st Company: John Shackleford, Captain; Doldzil Pace, 1st Lieut.; James Lamas, 2nd Lieut.

    2nd Company: Horatio Marbury, Captain; John Collins, 1st Lieut.; Edward B. Jenkins, 2nd Lieut.

    3rd Company: Richard P. White, Captain; John Lamkin, 1st Lieut.; Nicholas Meriwether, 2nd Lieut.

    4th Company: Peachey Bledsoe, Captain; Hayden Fryer, 1st Lieut.; John Bruce, 2nd Lieut.

    5th Company: John Booker, Captain; John Burnett, 1st Lieut.; Thomas Sturgis, 2nd Lieut.

    6th Company: Andrew Hays, Captain; Booker Tindall, 1st Lieut.; John Monk, 2nd Lieut.

    7th Company: Jesse Offutt, Captain; Matthew Duncan, 1st Lieut.; Neal Dougherty, 2nd Lieut.

    8th Company; John Cobb, Captain, William Few, Jr., 1st Lieut.; Gad W. Harrison, 2nd Lieut.

    9th Company: Benjamin Rees, Captain; Sampson Steel, 1st Lieut.; Fitz M. Hunt, 2nd Lieut.

    10th Company: L. Thomas Jones, Captain; William Douther, 1st Lieut.; John Travis, 2nd Lieut.

    11th Company: John Lawson, Captain; James Batley, 1st Lieut.; Thomas Jones, 2nd Lieut.

    12th Company: John Hatcher, Captain; Edward Vann, 1st Lieut.; Samuel Brady, 2nd Lieut.

- Note: Assuming each company had one hundred men, the above would mean that Columbia County had in 1790, 1200 men, of militia age, enrolled and subject to call.
- Judge Folks Huxford, Legal Notices in Early Ga. Newspapers 168-170.

Columbia County Militia Districts

1st District: From the mouth of Uchee Creek, then up same to Twiggs Road; thence along said road to the coutny line, then down the same to the Savannah River.

2nd District: From the mouth of the Great Kiokee, thence up said stream to Greenbrier Creek; thence up same to the road from Brownsboro to Kiokee Meeting-house; thence down said road by the Court-house to Uchee bridge; thence down the Uchee to the Savannah River.

3rd District: From the mouth of Little River up the same to Absalom Farrer's, thence with the road leading by Brownsboro to Greenbrier Creek, thence with the line of District #2 to the Savannah River.

4th District: From Scott's bridge on Little River, thence with the road leading by Ray's Mill to Greenbrier Creek; thence down said creek to the line of District #3, and thence on said line to Little River.

5th District: From Barnett's Bridge on Uchee Creek, thence up said creek to Twiggs Road, thence with the road to Tindall's Tavern; thence the road leading to Capt. Stevens' on the Kiokee, to Greenbrier Creek; thence down said creek to the line of District #2, thence that line to point of beginning.

6th District: Begin where the county line crosses Brier Creek, thence up said creek to the Iron Works, thence along the Augusta road to Pasley's old field; thence along Harris' old road to the line of District #5; thence with that line to Uchee Creek; thence with the Twiggs Road to the county line (or point of beginning).

7th District: Beginning at the Iron Works on Brier Creek, thence up said creek to the trading road, thence up said road to Jamerson's old place, thence with the road leading by the Baptist Meeting-house to Sweetwater, thence to John Davis' on the Quaker Road; thence down said road to Greenbrier Creek; thence down said creek to the line of Dist. #5; thence with that line to the line of Dist. #6, thence with that line to the Iron Works.

8th District: Begin at the mouth of Upton's Creek, thence up the said creek to the bridge at Wrightsborough, thence down the Quaker Road to Greenbrier

Creek; thence down said creek to line of District #4; thence that line to Little River.

9th District: Begin where the old Trading Road crosses Brier Creek, thence with the line of District #7 to the Quaker Road near John Davis', thence up said road to Wrightsborough, thence with the road leading by Benjamin Oliver's to the county line, thence down the same to point of beginning.

10th District: Begin at the mouth of Upton Creek, thence up said creek with the line of District #8 to the bridge at Wrightsborough, thence along the line of District #9 to the county line; thence up said line to William's Creek, thence down the same to Little Creek, thence to point of beginning.

11th District: All that part of the county between Brier Creek and Rocky Comfort.

12th District: All that part of the county between Rocky Comfort and the Ogeechee River.

"Dead on the Field of Honor"

The County's Men Who Were Killed in Action

1861-1973

J.F. Adams	Casey Carroll
John Q. Adams	J.Y. Carroll
R. Adams	W.J. Chamberlain
G. Adams	Hilman Cliatt
G. Anderson	Isaac Clieatt
A. Armstrong	Richard Cliatt
G.W. Arrington	William Cliatt
Wilson Baker	G. Cobb
G.W. Barber	J.S. Coldwell
C. Baylis	Amos Corley
T.C. Bennett	F.M. Darsey
J.M. Benson	J. Eubanks
N.C. Benton	B. Fitzgerald
N.E. Benton	H.E. Flanigan
J.T. Binion	J. Garnet
J.T. Blackston	William B. Garrett
J.W. Blackston	B.F. Gay
A. Blackstone	Henry Gay
B. Blackstone	John Gay
Lee Blackstone	Thomas Gay
W.M. Blanchard	J. Green
William Blanchard	William G. Green
Blichington	S. Guy
B. Blichington	R.C. Hatcher
J.J. Bond	R.A.L. Hatrick
J.W. Bonner	J. Henry
William Bonner	T.T. Hobbs
James Boyd	S. Holliman
Robert Boyd	N.S. Hubbard
T.B. Buck	Dennis Inglett
A.J. Bugg	H.M. Johnson
John Bugg	R.T. Johnosn
D. Burnside	A. Johnson
J. Burnside	O.H. Johnson

J.W. Jones
James Jones
S.E. Jones
C. Knox
R. Knox
T.C. Lamkin
E.T. Langford
J.R. Langford
W.B. Langston
Sam Lokey
John G. Luke
E.C. Magruder
G.R. Magruder
O. Magruder
H.C. Massengale
A.D. McGahee
J. McGahee
M. McGahee
R. McGahee
J.M. Miles
F.P. Moore
H. Moore
C.O. Morris
F. Morris
John Morris
L.B. Morris
S.H. Morris
Elisha Newman
Thomas Newman
Wade Newman
C. Palmer
A.W. Parham
Thomas Perrin
John Pond
J.W. Porter
A.C. Prather
B.F. Prather
W.H. Pullin
A.J. Reese
J.J. Reese
J.M. Reynolds
H. Rooks
G. Rooks

John Scott
William Scott
J. Shaw
J.W. Shields
W.B. Shockley
W.M. Sills
A.L. Simms
A.C. Sims
B.F. Smith
G. Smith
J. Smith
S. Standford
W.A. Standford
L.T.Stanton
J.H. Sturgis
J.M. Sutherland
P. Sutherland
Tankersley
R.B. Tankersley
S. Tillery
Willaim Tillery
J. Tillery
J.V. Underwood
J.D. Walker
O. Walker
J.A. Wall
Henry Ward
Jesse Ward
L.W. Ward
W.M. Watson
V.G. Weathers
A. Welch
C.C. Welch
J. Welch
J.W. Wheeler
R.B. Wheeler
William Wheeler
George Whitefield
Tyler Whitefield
J. Whitten
A.S. Wilkerson
D.T. Wilson
G.W. Wilson

David Winson
T.A. Wynn
D. Yarborough

G.L. Young
J.D. Young

WWI – 1914-1918

Barney Bivens
John Burnett

Doughty Jansen
Selwyn Williamson

WWII – 1941-1945

Robert Bryan
Daniel Cason
Perry L. Crapps
John B. Crawford
Walter J. Fullbright, Jr.
Earl W. Huff
Frank Kauffman
Fred Malone

Emmel Winslow Mundy
Clyde Pardue, Jr.
Harold E. Reid
Herber Rochester
Thomas W. Smith
Charlie C. Snellings
Willie S. Sweatman
George R. Vaughn

Korea – 1950-1953

Corydon W. Benton
Edward D. Hunter

Delmas McNeal

Vietnam – 1965-1973

Harold Crawford
James Lee Davis
Joseph Daniel Goodale, Jr.
G. Wayne Inglett
William Thomas John

Fred W. Mitchell, Jr.
Rogers Pullins, Jr.
Carl Andrew Olsen
Nathan Thomas
Edward Thurman

Columbia County History Bibliography

Manuscript Collections

Clements Library, Ann Arbor, Michigan

Shelburne Papers:
Dispatch of Royal Governor James Wright, 1766.
Letter of Dr. Thomas Tayor, 1776.

Columbia County Courthouse:

Plat Book A

Deed Book Z

Emory University:

Ignatius Few Papers

Georgia Department of Archives and History:

George W. Crawford Papers

William Few, Jr. Papers

University of Georgia Library, Hargrett Rm.,

E. Merton Coulter Collection

Keith-Jones Papers (Relates to a Columbia County Plantation

Abraham Baldwin Papers

Moses Waddel Papers

National Archives and Records

Pension Claim S. 8167

Bibliography

Richmond County Courthouse
Superior Court Records 1791-1792

University of North Carolina, Southern Historical Collection
Moses Waddel Letter

Newspapers

Albany (Georgia) Herald

Augusta Chronicle

Augusta Chronicle And Sentinel

Augusta Chronicle And Gazette Of State Of Georgia

Augusta Constitutionalist

Columbia News

Columbia News-Times

Columbia Sentinel

Macon Telegraph

Southern Sentinel And Gazette

Official Publications

Acts And Resolutions Of The General Assembly Of Georgia 1825-1900

Bibliography

Candler, Allen D., comp. <u>The Colonial Records Of The State Of Georgia</u>. 26 volumes. Atlanta: Printers vary, 1904-1916

_____, <u>The Revolutionary Records Of The State Of Georgia</u>. 3 volumes. Atlanta: Franklin-Turner, 1908

<u>Cultural Resources Survey, Thurmond Lake, Mcduffie And Columbia Counties</u>. Washington, D.C.: USDA, 1976

<u>Harlem's Community Development Plan</u>. Atlanta: Department of Community Development, 1977.

Henderson, Lillian, comp. <u>Roster Of The Confederate Soldiers Of Georgia</u>. 6 volumes. Hapeville, Georgia: Longino and Porter, 1956-1960.

<u>Journal Of The Convention At Milledgeville And Savannah 1861</u>. Milledgeville: Boughton, Nisbet, and Barnes, 1861.

<u>Journal Of The Senate Of The State Of Georgia</u>. Atalanta: various publishers, 1848.

<u>Minutes Of The Annual Conferences Of The Methodist Episcopal Church South</u>. 2 volumes. Nashville: MECS Publishing House, 1858-1865.

<u>Report Of The Comptroller General Of The State Of Georgia</u>. Atlanta: various publishers, 1872

<u>Soil Survey Of Columbia, Mcduffie And Warren Counties</u>. Washington, D.C.: USDA, 1967,
State Historic Preservation Office,
Department of Natural Resources, Atlanta, Georgia.

<u>United States Bureau Of The Census, 1790-1970</u>.

Other Printed Sources

Anderson, David and Kenneth Sassaman, The Paleoindian And Early Archaic Southeast. Tuscaloosa: University of Alabama Press, 1996.

Anderson, David. The Savannah River Chiefdoms. Tuscaloosa: University of Alabama Press, 1994.

Abilene Baptist Church. Strength For Today Bright Hope For Tomorrow. Franklin, Tennessee: Providence House, 1999.

Barclay, Wade C. Early American Methodism, 1769 –1844. II New York: New York: Board of Missions and Church Extension of the Methodist Church, 1949.

Bartram, William. The Travels Of William Bartram. Edited by Francis Harper. New Haven, Connecticut, 1958.

Bell, W.A. Missions And Cooperation Of The Methodist Episcopal Church South With The Colored Methodist Episcopal Church. Nashville: Commission on Cooperation and Counsel, 1933.

Blackard, William C., Thomas Huckabee, and Gerald J. Smith. Columbia County, Georgia. Charleston: Arcadia Press, 2000.

Bryan, T. Conn. Confederate Georgia. Athens: University of Georgia, 1953.

Burr, Virgina, ed. "The Secret Eye": The Journal Of Ella G. Clanton Thomas 1848-1889. Chapel Hill: University of North Carolina Press, 1990.

Bibliography

Cartledge, Tony W. "Samuel Cartledge: Colonial 'Saul of Tarsus,'" <u>Viewpoints Georgia Baptist History 8</u> (1982), 13-32.

Casey, H.R. "Reminiscences," <u>Columbia Sentinel, 1883</u>, various pages.

Cashin, Edward. Ed. <u>A Wilderness Still In The Cradle Of Nature: Frontier Georgia</u>. Savannah: Beehive, 1994.

_____, <u>Colonial Augusta</u>: "Key of the Indian Country" Macon: Mercer University Press, 1986.

_____, <u>The King's Ranger</u>. Athens: University of Georgia Press, 1989.

Cherpak, Evelyn. "David Bushnell," <u>American National Biography 4</u>, Eds. John Garraty and Mark Carnes. New York: Oxford, 1999.

Cimbala, Paul. "On the Front Line of Freedom: Freedmen's Bureau Officers and Agents in Reconstruction Georgia," <u>Georgia Historical Quarterly 76</u> (Fall 1992), 590-614.

Claflin, William. "The Stallings Island Mound," <u>Peabody Museum Papers XIV</u> New York: Kraus, 1922.

Cohen, Robert. "Public Schools in Hard Times: Letters to Eleanor and Franklin Roosevelt, 1933-1942," <u>Georgia Historical Quarterly 72</u> (Spring 1998), 121-150.

Coit, Margaret. "Moses Waddel: A Light in the Wilderness," <u>Georgia Review 5</u> (Spring 1951), 34-47.

Coulter, E. Merton. "Ante Bellum Academy Movement in Georgia," <u>Georgia Historical Quarterly 5</u> (1921), 11-42.

_____, Georgia: A Short History. Chapel Hill: University of North Carolina Press, 1947.

_____, Old Petersburg And The Broad River Valley. Athens: University of Georgia Press, 1965.

_____, Ed. "Waddel's Memoir," Georgia Historical Quarterly 8 (1924), 306-320.

Crawford, George. "Cotton, Land, and Sustenance: Toward the Limits of Abundance in the Late Antebellum Georgia," Georgia Historical Quarterly 62 (Summer 1988), 215-247.

Crawford, James M. "Yuchi Phonology," International Journal Of American Linguistics 39 (1973), 173-179.

Davis, Robert, Jr. Quaker Records In Georgia: Wrightsborough 1772-1793 And Friendsborough 1771-1777. Roswell: Wolfe, 1986.

Davis, William C., ed. The Confederate Generals, 4. Harrisburg: National Historical Society, 1991.

Drago, Edmund L. Black Politicians And Reconstruction In Georgia: A Splendid Failure. Baton Rouge: Louisiana State University Press, 1982.

_____, "Georgia's First Black Voter Registrars During Reconstruction." Georgia Historical Quarterly 78 (Winter 1994), 760-793.

Duggan, M.L. Educational Survey Of Heard County. Atlanta: Department of Education, 1917.

Bibliography

Duncan, Russell. <u>Freedom's Shore: Tunis Campbell And The Georgia Freedmen</u>. Athens: University of Georgia Press, 1986.

Elliott, Daniel. "Archaeology and Historical Geography of the Savannah River Floodplain near Augusta, Georgia," <u>Laboratory Of Archaeology</u> Series Report No. 22. Athens, University of Georgia, 1981.

Fruth, Florence. <u>Some Descendants Of Richard Few Of Chester County, Pennsylvania</u>. New York: McClain, 1977.

Gardner, David T. "Henry Lewis Benning: Confederate General." M.A. Thesis, Auburn University, 1998.

Gardner, Robert G. "African American Institutions in Georgia." <u>Viewpoints Georgia Baptist History 16</u> (1998), 7-30.

_____, Mary Overby, and Charles Walker. "Historical Listing of Baptist Associations in Georgia, 1784-1994." <u>Viewpoints Georgia Baptist History 14</u> (1994), 23-44.

<u>Georgia Courthouse Manual</u>. Atlanta: Georgia Department of Community Affairs, 1992.

Harris, Waldo III and James D. Mosteller. <u>Georgia's First Continuing Baptist Church</u>. College Park, Georgia: N&R Printing, 1997.

Harwell, Richard. "Erskine Caldwell: Georgia Cracker Worldclass," <u>The Atlanta Historical Journal 26</u> (Winter 1982-83), 5-18.

Hitz, Alex. "Georgia Bounty Grants." Georgia Historical Quarterly 38 (1954).

Holley, Thomas. Company F Thomson Guards Tenth Regiment Georgia Volunteers Army Of Northern Virginia Confederate States Of America. Fernandina, Florida: Wolfe, 2000.

Hudson, Charles. The Southeastern Indians. Knoxville: University of Tennessee Press, 1976.

Hvidt, Chrisian, ed. Von Reck's Voyage. Savannah: Beehive, 1990.

Jones, Charles Colcock, Jr. Antiquities of The Southern Indians, Particularly Of The Georgia Tribes. New York: Appleton, 1873.

Kane, Sharyn and Richard Keaton. Beneath These Waters. Washington, D.C.: National Park Service, 1993.

Killion, Ronald G. ed. "Reminiscences of the 'Peculiar Institution'," Sandlapper 5 (October 1972), 49-55.

Knight, L.L. Reminiscences of Famous Georgians. Atlanta: Franklin-Turner, 1908.

Lamplugh, George. Farewell to the Revolution Georgia in 1785." Georgia Historical Quarterly 56 (Fall 1972), 387-403.

_____, "William Few's Brownsborough Plan." Richmond County History 5 (Winter 1973), 40-45.

Lazenby, Jean. "History of Columbia County Schools." M.A. Thesis, Atlanta University, 1980.

Bibliography

Litchtenstein, Alex. "Good Roads and Chain Gangs in the Progressive South: 'The Negro Convict Is a Slave.'" The Journal Of Southern History 59 (February 1993), 85-110.

Marshall, Dan. "Rare Plants Thrive at Heggies Rock." Albany Herald, 1999.

Martin, Hugh, Ed. Selections From The Journal Of John Wesley. London: SCM Press, 1955.

Miller, Charles. "The Lake Springs Site, Columbia County." American Antiquities 15, 438-519.

Miller, John, "Evans Baptist Church. 1930-1980," n.p.n.d.

Miller, Robert Moats. "Southern White Protestantism and the Negro, 1865-1965." The Negro In The South Since 1865: Selected Essays In American Negro History. New York: Negro Universities Press. 1966.

Mims, Edwin. "Paul Hamilton Hayne." Library Of Southern Literature 5. Atlanta: Martin and Hoyt, 1907.

Moore, Patricia Ann. "History of Harlem Georgia." Historic Bicentennial Zip Code Directory And Daily Date Book. Harlem: North Harlem Elementary P.T.A., 1976, 1-9.

Moore, Rayburn. A Man Of Letters In The Nineteenth Century South: Selected Letters Of Paul Hamilton Hayne. Baton Rouge: Louisiana State University Press, 1982.

Mosely, Charlton. "Latent Klanism in Georgia 1890-1915," Georgia Historical Quarterly 56 (Fall 1972), 365-386.

Bibliography

Newby, Idus. The South: A History. New York: Holt, Rinehart and Winston, 1978.

Northern, W.J. Ed. Men Of Mark In Georgia 6 Volumes. Atlanta: Caldwell, 1910.

Oakes, James. The Ruling Race: A History Of American Slaveholders. New York: Vintage, 1983.

Orr, Dorothy. A History Of Education In Georgia. Chapel Hill: University of North Carolina Press, 1950.

Phillips, U.B. ed. The Correspondence Of Robert Toombs, Alexander H. Stephens, And Howell Cobb. II Washington, D.C.: Government Printing Office, 1913.

Pollard, Leslie. Complaint To The Lord: Historical Perspectives Of The African American Elderly. Selingsgrove, New York: Susquehanna University Press, 1996.

Pope, G.D., Jr. Ocmulgee. Washington, D.C.: National Park Service, 1940.

Ramsdell, Charles. "The Natural Limits of Slave Expansion." Mississippi Valley Historical Review 16 (1929), 151-171.

Range, Willard. A Century Of Georgia Agriculture 1850-1950. Athens: University of Georgia Press, 1954.

Redford, A.H. History Of Methodism In Kentucky, I. Nashville: Southern Methodist Publishing House, 1910.

Robertson, Heard. Loyalism In Revolutionary Georgia. Atlanta: Georgia Committee for the National Bicentennial Celebration and the Georgia Department of Education, 1978.

Rodgers, Margaret. Historical Landmarks And Legends Of Columbia County. Appling, Georgia: Historical Society, 1976.

Ruddy, Kathy B. A Cornerstone Of Life In The Village Of Grovetown: The First 60 Years Of Grovetown (Methodist) Episcopal Church, South, Grovetown, Georgia 1880-1940. Privately published, 1999.

Sassaman, Kenneth. "Stallings: The Rise and Fall of a Hunting Gathering Society." Legacy I (July 1996), 6-15.

Sassaman, Kenneth and David Anderson. Archaeology Of The Mid-Holocene Southeast. Gainesville: University Press Florida, 1996.

Scott, Ralph, Jr. "The Quaker Settlement at Wrightsborough." Georgia Historical Quarterly 56 (1972), 211-223.

Schweitzer, George K. Georgia Genealogical Research. Privately published, 1995.

Sherwood, Adiel. Gazateer Of The State Of Georgia. Atlanta: Richards, 1827 and 1829.

Smith, George Gilman. Life And Letters Of James Osgood Andrew. New York: Trow's, 1882.

_____, A Hundred Years Of Methodism In Augusta. Augusta, Georgia: Richards and Shavers, 1898.

Smith, Gerald J. Letters, Diaries, And Reminiscences Of The Union And The Confederacy. Murfreesboro, Tennessee: Ambassador, 1995.

_____, "Smite Them Hip And Thigh!" Georgia Methodist Ministers In The Confederate Military. Murfreesboro: Ambassador, 1993.

Stearns, Charles. The Black Man Of The South And The Rebels Or, The Characteristics Of The Former And The Recent Outrages Of The Latter. New York: American News Company, 1872.

Stevens, O.B. Georgia, Historical And Industrial. Atlanta: Harrison, 1901.

Steiner, Robert R. "Prehistoric Settlement, Big Kiokee Creek, Columbia County." American Association For The Advancement Of Scientific Proceedings. 1899.

Swanton, John R. The Early History Of The Creek Indians Bulletin #73. Washington, D.C.: Government Printing Office, 1922; Reprint, 1998.

Thompson, Mildred. Reconstruction In Georgia. Atlanta: Cherokee, 1971.

Turner, Julie. "Harlem, Ga.: Influences on Early Development and Growth." Richmond County History 16 (Summer 1984), 11-20.

Wade, John Donald. Augustus Baldwin Longstreet: A Study Of The Development Of Culture In The South. New York: MacMillan, 1924.

Walker, Alice, comp. Personal Name Index To The Augusta Chronicle 4 Volumes. Augusta: Augusta-Richmond County Library, 1988.

Bibliography

Websters <u>American Military Biographies</u>. Springfield, Massachusetts: G.&C. Merriam Company, 1978.

White, George. <u>Historical Collections Of Georgia</u>. New York: Russell, 1854.

Wicander, Reed and James Monroe. <u>Historical Geology: Evolution Of The Earth And Life In Time</u>. New York: West, 1989.

Electronic Sources

http://www.desktop-university.com/columbiahistory/

http://www.columbiacntyga.com/

http://www.fisher.lib.virginia.edu/ (for the United States Historical Census Data)

http://www.galileo.peachnet.edu/

Private Collections

Lallie Dozier Benkoski

Dan Marshall

Gerald J. Smith

Josie Dozier

Charles Lord

Bibliography

INDEX

H

Savannah · 2, 6, 9, 10, 17, 19,
20, 21, 22, 26, 33, 35, 41,
44, 54, 55, 56, 57, 59, 79,
85, 95, 107, 119, 121, 138,
150, 157, 158, 159, 161,
162
Savannah River Site · 54, 119
Saw Dust · 91
Sawdust · 115
scalawag · 47
scapegoat · 46
Secession · 38, 49
Second Mount Moriah · 100
Sell · 21
Sentinel · 49, 58, 88, 116,
156
Separate Baptists · 23
settlement · 23, 56, 58, 94,
115, 118
Sewallville · 111
sharecropping · 46
Sharon · 96
Shelter belts · 130
Shepherd · 101
Sherman · 44, 52, 110
Sherwood · 23, 29, 56, 58,
67, 80, 113, 124, 165
Shiloh · 90, 91
Simms · 121, 140
Smith · 3, 39, 55, 60, 74, 85,
91, 107, 158, 165, 167
Smith Grove · 74
Societies · 105
Solid Rock · 74, 100
Sons of Liberty · 24, 57

South Columbia Elementary ·
77
South Harlem Elementary ·
74, 77
Southern Sentinel And
Gazette · 64, 156
sports · 129
Spring Grove · 74
St. John's Methodist · 91
St. Paul's Parish · 20, 21, 23
stagecoach · 114
Stallings · 7, 8, 9, 10, 16,
159, 165
State Department of
Education · 72
Stearns · 46, 47, 60, 61, 69,
72, 166
Steiner Grove · 74, 100
Stephens · 37, 38, 58, 59, 164
Stevens · 30, 51, 52, 61, 77,
117, 166
Stevens Creek XE "Creek"
XE "Water and Rivers"
Elementary · 77
Story · 89, 107, 133
Strom Thurmond Lake · 3, 55
Submarine · 67
Sudan Industries · 128
Sullivan · 103
Summerville · 137
Swaminarayan Temple · 101

T

Tabor · 91

U

V

W

Y

Printed in the United States
1841